Cutting Edge Cricket

CONTENTS

PART III The Practice and Playing Environment

FOREWORD

On behalf of Cricket Australia, I am delighted to introduce *Cutting Edge Cricket*, a book that brings together the thoughts of some of Australian cricket's most innovative minds.

Cricket's vision is to be Australia's favourite sport and this book aims to support that objective through two of Cricket Australia's five strategic pillars: to 'thrive at the elite level' through the performance of the Australian men's and women's teams and to 'substantially increase sustainable participation in cricket' by enhancing the quality of the cricket experience at all levels.

Resources such as this book are important tools as Australian cricket strives to remain a leader in world sport, reinforcing and celebrating cricket's unique place in the Australian community and the world. We know you will enjoy this resource, which is rich with successful tips from many Australian cricket champions who have underpinned our recent success.

We believe this book will help coaches create a better cricket environment that is consistent with Cricket Australia's Game Development strategy to grow the game in the areas of female, indigenous, multicultural, disability and entry-level participation.

Finally, thank you to co-authors Dr Frank Pyke and Dr Ken Davis who, along with Human Kinetics and Cricket Australia, have delivered a book rich in knowledge and experience.

Long live cricket!

James Sutherland
Chief Executive Officer
Cricket Australia
www.cricket.com.au

ACKNOWLEDGMENTS

The authors would like to thank Andrew Larratt from Cricket Australia and Chris Halbert from Human Kinetics Australia for developing the concept of this project and for their dedicated commitment in bringing it to fruition.

PHOTO CREDITS

INTRODUCTION

During the last 50 years, the world of high performance sport has changed significantly. With the advent of modern technology and global television coverage, it has become both highly commercial and highly competitive. Outstanding athletes now command large salaries and sponsorships and have to perform in front of big crowds and television audiences. They are an integral part of the entertainment industry. Cricket is no exception.

Back in the era of Bradman's 'Invincibles', cricketers were amateurs and played first-class and Test matches, each lasting several days. When they went on tour to overseas countries, they reached their destination by passenger ship. Today's international players fly around the world to fulfil what is now a hectic schedule of Test and limited over matches. There has also been a significant increase in the number of countries involved in cricket. In short, the highest level of the game has become international big business.

The first major influence in broadening the scope and appeal of the game in Australia was the commencement of World Series Cricket in the late 1970s. Using a white ball and a 50-over day/night format, a competition was staged annually between international teams and shown on prime time television. Since then, One Day International cricket has continued to be an important part of Australian sport during the summer months. The second major influence occurred recently with the development of the even shorter Twenty20 format and the establishment of the Indian Premier League.

Demands on Players

Today's busy schedule of Test, one-day and half-day matches has heightened the competitiveness among cricket-playing nations and placed more pressure on players to perform under a variety of formats and playing conditions. With a heavier overall workload and less time for recovery, players also need to be selected and trained differently. This has led to sport science and medicine becoming key ingredients in modern training programs, enabling the responses of individual players to be closely monitored to preserve their long-term health and performance capabilities.

Preparing a cricketer for the game today is a far cry from what was required 30 years ago before the one-day version of the game became popular. And it will probably be different again tomorrow as the adrenaline-charged world in which we live demands more entertainment, such as that offered by the Twenty20 format. This trend places greater pressure on the coach and the captain to manage the players during both their off-field preparation and on-field performance. They must consider not only the busy playing schedule but also the many skills required to play the various forms of the game. Modern players need to have a versatile skill set that enables them to do this.

In the past, teams included players who could either bat or bowl but were inept in the field. This is no longer possible, particularly in shorter versions of the game. Having athletic, multi-skilled fielders who can sprint, catch, dive and throw is now a fundamental requirement. Saving runs is as important as making them.

Success Factors

Within any cricketing country the importance of success on the international stage is passed down from the highest level of the sport to youth and junior teams. Achieving success at any level depends on many factors including the talent of the players involved, the quality of their coaches and support staff, their access to modern training facilities and equipment, their opportunity to participate in intensive competition and the culture of the environment in which they train and compete.

A winning team culture requires all parties to make an enthusiastic and passionate commitment to achieving excellence. By definition, such a culture embraces a strong work ethic, innovation and continual learning, teamwork and exemplary and ethical behaviour. Everyone involved must share the same set of values.

Attributes of the Best

Certain defining qualities of our best players clearly set them apart from the rest. These qualities are what it takes to succeed, not only in cricket but in other areas of life. Together they address the strength of the body, mind and spirit.

Good cricketers must have a blend of technical skill, fitness and psychological attributes that are best suited to their specific roles in the game. Among other qualities, a batsman must have good eye–hand coordination, a fast bowler must have muscular power and endurance and a wicketkeeper must be quick and agile. Although many of these characteristics are inherited, they can also be improved by physical and mental training.

Natural talent needs to be matched by an intense passion for the sport. Our best players love to practice and love to play. It fires their souls. Only players who are passionate about what they are doing are likely to make the commitment to engage in intensive training and succeed in competition. The passion for cricket is fuelled by an enjoyment of physical activity and the personal fulfillment associated with achieving success. In this respect, passion depends on the quality of the experience players have had in the sport throughout their lives. Encouragement from their family, friends, teachers and coaches is fundamental in this process.

In any area of life, successful people have a very strong work ethic. The same applies to cricket. There is no substitute for hard work, which often means the difference between being good and being the best. Achieving success requires commitment, dedication, self-discipline and sacrifice. Again, the willingness to work hard seems to come naturally to those who have been encouraged from an early age, but others have to learn it. It is the role of the coach to instil this mindset in all members of the training squad, because, as is often said, 'hard work will beat talent if talent doesn't work hard'.

Although it is vital for our best players to have natural talent, a passion for their sport and a strong work ethic, they also need knowledgeable coaches and service personnel to provide specialised support in sport science and medicine, strength and conditioning and education and career development. Collectively, their role is to ensure that the cricketer adheres to an individualised training and competition plan that contains clear and realistic short- and long-term goals.

Ultimately, however, cricketers must become self-determining and take responsibility for their own training and performance. This quality sets champions apart. Coaches need to encourage players to put themselves in charge of their own destiny, rather than remain dependent on others. This is part of the development process. They should work to a plan and set themselves short-term goals to focus on specific aspects of their performance that they feel need improving. The plan should also include long-term goals oriented towards achieving their desired outcomes.

Cricketers should have balance in their lives and develop personal skills and careers beyond sport. This is based on the understanding that the complementary development of the mind and body is performance enhancing. There are many examples of champion athletes who have also been successful in other areas of their lives. Moreover, professional players need to prepare for life beyond cricket.

A quality that stands out in the best players is their mental toughness during matches. The margin between winning and losing is often very small, and success is determined by the capacity to perform under pressure. Meeting the challenges associated with performing in adverse conditions against quality opponents requires great mental strength and resolve. It is often said that when the going gets tough, the tough get going. Although this mindset comes easier to some than to others, developing competitive toughness is all part of the development process. Athletes learn to respond in a positive way to the challenging circumstances confronting them.

Very few players reach the top of this sport without experiencing some form of setback that retards their progress, such as a crisis in their lives, a serious illness or injury or non-selection at a vital time. The capacity to overcome these roadblocks and return to the game even stronger and smarter and better able to cope with adversity is a quality of champions. They possess an abundance of perseverance and resilience.

The best players are true believers in themselves and do not even contemplate failure. They have a positive 'can do' attitude that leaves no room for uncertainty and self-doubt. Their view is that this mindset, backed up with actions, will give them the competitive edge required to succeed.

Outstanding players take great pride in their performance. That pride shows in how they approach their training, their pre-match preparation and their performances in matches. They simply want to be as good as they can be every time they appear on the big stage. They go about their business in a way that is inspirational for others.

The objective of this book is to provide ways and means of improving the daily training environment of cricketers so that they can become their best, and for some, ultimately, the best. Included are not only some of the best drills to improve their batting, bowling, fielding and wicketkeeping skills but also the best means of physically and mentally preparing them to perform. Drills and practices are highlighted with green and yellow headings. This book also covers best practice strategies for captains and coaches to follow in leading and managing a team. This is a big challenge in a sport that has a greater individual focus than many other team sports do. However, to maximise player development, everyone must be aligned to the team's core values. This is what effective leadership is all about.

In meeting this objective, we have compiled the thoughts and practices of some of the most successful and influential people who have been involved in Australian cricket. Their collective purpose is to add to our knowledge about a game that has enthralled our nation during its summer life and inspired our youth to play hard but fair and be challenged by the desire to become the best.

PART I

Player Preparation

The first part of this book is essentially about preparing the mind and the body for the uncertainties and challenges that are inherent in cricket. Being called upon at a moment's notice to go in to bat, and then remaining there for three or four hours in the hot and uncomfortable conditions often experienced in a summer match, is a unique test of the mind, body and spirit.

The fundamental message in the first part of chapter 1, Physical Preparation, is that adhering to established principles should give each player the best training prescription to maximise performance. Close monitoring of player workloads, particularly those of pace bowlers, as well as the specific health and safety of all players, provides some safeguard against them suffering from debilitating injuries and illnesses. Injury and illness prevention is a priority, particularly for teams travelling long distances to fulfil busy playing schedules. Various exercise routines used in warm-up, cool-down and rehabilitation programs are also provided in this chapter.

Mental skills programs are described in detail in chapter 2, Mental Preparation. The mind is the body's control box, and if it emits positive and focused signals, the body will respond with power, skill and precision. However, for this to occur, both the mind and the body must follow carefully planned and individualised mental and physical preparation programs. Above all, they must work together. The first concept covered is mental toughness. The best players have a number of attributes that fit this description, including self-belief, self-motivation, resilience and the capacity to thrive under pressure. The chapter lists cricket-oriented indicators of mental toughness. The practical methods of learning the mental skills required in cricket such as visualisation, focusing and dealing with mistakes are also given high priority. The process by which batters and wicketkeepers learn how to anticipate the speed and direction of a ball being bowled at them adds an interesting and valuable final dimension to the chapter.

This section of the book also highlights the valuable contributions of the various professional service providers to player development. These include the physician, physiotherapist, psychologist and members of the strength and conditioning staff, all of whom work with the head coach to ensure that all players are engaged in a physical and mental preparation program that meets their immediate and specific needs.

CHAPTER 1

Physical Preparation

As with any sport, optimum performance in cricket requires players to possess a number of well-developed physical attributes. These include endurance, speed, power, flexibility and balance. Achieving these depends on following scientifically based training principles, preventing some of the common injuries and illnesses experienced during the match and recovering quickly from any that are encountered.

Pace bowlers must have each of these attributes developed to a high level. Depending on the time spent at the crease and in the field, the same can be said for batters and fielders. However, because all players must be fully prepared for any circumstances that might arise, a well-rounded program is essential for every member of the team. Most important, because each player has unique attributes, the program should be aimed at overcoming individual limitations.

Principles of Training

A number of principles make up the prescription of training programs, including progressive overload, recovery, specificity and individuality. These principles provide the basis on which cricket coaches can design programs to prevent injury and enhance performance.

Progressive Overload

To improve their fitness, players must be subjected to training loads beyond those to which they are normally accustomed. This will create in them a need to adapt to meet the extra demands. Overload can be achieved by increasing the frequency and volume of training as well as the intensity of the load. The challenge for the coach is to produce in the player a need to adapt without going too far and becoming chronically fatigued. Hence, training should begin slowly and progress gradually. For example, longer, slower running provides a useful endurance fitness foundation for the more intensive short-interval sprints that are required to prepare for fast bowling or running between wickets.

Sudden and large increases in volume or intensity can be counterproductive. In the early stages, weekly increases should therefore be kept below 10 per cent. It is also important to alternate harder sessions with easier ones. At the elite level of the game, GPS technology is now used to monitor the output of players so that the intensity of training can be adjusted according to their heart rate and subjective responses to the workout.

Recovery

The overload required to elicit a training response is linked closely to the recovery permitted between training sessions or cycles. The coach should seek daily subjective feedback from players to gauge their response to the training so that, if necessary, the load can be adjusted. Weekly saliva tests to evaluate hormone levels also provide a guide to the level of stress that players are experiencing. Players need an adequate level of protein and carbohydrate in the diet and should promptly replace the fluid lost in sweating. Recovery is also assisted by light exercise and stretching, relaxation techniques, massage and cold water therapy and good sleeping habits.

Specificity

The most appropriate training regime is one that closely simulates the movements and energy systems used in cricket. However, rather than have players just play the game, where the work intensity may sometimes be too low to obtain a significant training effect, coaches should design cricket-related activities such as interval sprints to simulate the approach of fast bowlers and running between wickets for batters. For example, fast bowlers can complete a series of 25- to 30-metre sprints at about 90 per cent of top speed with 15-second recovery periods between them. Sets of six to eight sprints should be interspersed with 60- to 90-second breaks between sets.

JUSTIN LANGER uses a similar interval sprint format with shuttle runs to enhance his batting fitness. He places cones at the end of the pitch and completes 100 runs while imagining that a series of shots have been played. This might involve running a four after a straight drive, followed by a single for a shot behind square leg and then a two from a cover drive. Again, the practice is designed to simulate the circumstances likely to be encountered in a match.

Individuality

Group training never provides the best training for each player in the squad. Individuals have unique fitness, skill and mental attributes; lifestyles and work commitments; and responsibilities in the team. Their training programs should reflect these differences. Prematch warm-up and postmatch recovery routines should also reflect these differences because what may be essential for a fast bowler, for example, may not be as necessary for a fielder.

TIP In addition to participating in team drills, each member of the team needs the opportunity during a practice session to spend time overcoming any specific physical limitations. This will help them round out their profile of physical attributes and enhance their on-field performance.

Common Cricket Injuries and Illnesses

Injuries have become increasingly common in modern cricket. Fast bowlers are most affected as a result of the workload imposed on them during what is now a busy national and international playing schedule. The high intensity of activity in Twenty20 cricket also has an effect on the injury rates sustained by batters and fielders, although the limit on overs is helpful for bowlers. In international cricket, the potential for illness is high as a result of the need for players to travel long distances and live and play in foreign and often hot and humid environments.

During the past 10 years a number of reports from Cricket Australia medical personnel, compiled by Dr. **JOHN ORCHARD** and others, document the common injuries and illnesses being incurred at national and international levels of the game. Gathering survey information is part of a systematic process of injury and illness prevention that also involves identifying risk factors and implementing strategies to reduce the likelihood of these problems occurring.

Cricket Australia's 2008 injury report shows that there has been an overall increase in the number of injuries sustained, due mainly to an increase in the number of playing days in domestic cricket with the expansion of Twenty20 cricket.

Fast bowlers have the highest incidence of injury. The most common injuries are side and groin strains and ankle impingement injuries from landing on the front leg. In elite senior Australian cricket recently there has been a reduced incidence of lower back stress injuries. The authors suggest that this may be due to the preventative work being done to eliminate one of their main causes: a mixed bowling action in which the hips and shoulders are not aligned during the delivery stride. However, although the number of lower back injuries may be less among senior fast bowlers, young fast bowlers continue to have high incidences of these injuries.

Fielders experience shoulder tendon injuries from overuse and throwing while off balance. Such injuries are also more common among spin bowlers than pace bowlers. Fielders and batsmen incur hamstring and calf strains from sprinting in the outfield or between wickets. Because only four overs can be bowled by any one player in Twenty20 cricket, fewer bowling injuries have been reported in this form of the game than in longer formats. However, there is a higher incidence of batting and fielding injuries due to the elevated intensity of play.

In general, it has become clear that the increase in cricket injuries is linked primarily to an increase in workload. As Orchard and others have suggested, the incidence of injuries will continue to increase if Twenty20 cricket matches are scheduled without any reduction in the number of other matches on the annual calendar. The cumulative effect of a busy international and domestic schedule involving all forms of the game is potentially debilitating, particularly for fast bowlers.

Heat strain and exhaustion are commonly encountered in a summer sport such as cricket because players can become dehydrated while exercising in hot and humid environments. Teams travelling to overseas countries, particularly in the Indian subcontinent, can experience food poisoning as well as viral infections that can spread quickly among members of the playing squad. There is also the challenge of coping with a prolonged period in an aircraft and suffering from jet lag upon arrival at a distant destination.

Injury Prevention

Injury prevention must be a strong theme of any fitness program, particularly during the early stages before muscle groups are properly conditioned. Australian team physiotherapist **ALEX KOUNTOURIS** recommends a multi-factorial approach to injury prevention. This requires screening players at the outset for any predisposition to injury, including muscle inflexibility; muscle weakness; poor bowling, throwing or running mechanics; and any shortfalls in the levels of fitness required for the game. He is a strong advocate for an individualised approach to player preparation.

Players' workloads must be closely monitored by coaches because both too little and too much can increase the potential for injury. The training load of bowlers depends on how much work each is required to do and is capable of doing in a match. Pace bowler Brett Lee and leg spinner Shane Warne perform completely different tasks, while Brett Lee and Shaun Tait are completely different fast bowlers. These players' training programs should reflect these differences.

In recent years, a lot of attention has been given to preventing injuries in fast bowlers. Dennis Lillee was diagnosed with the first documented case of lumbar stress fractures among international fast bowlers. In his article on fast bowlers and the modern game in the 1998 *Wisden Cricketers Almanack*, he attributed the high incidence of injuries among fast bowlers in international cricket to the increased workload they endure during what has become a hectic playing schedule. To lengthen their careers, he suggested the following three solutions:

- Monitor bowlers' workloads closely, placing strict limits on the number of balls delivered in a particular time period, along the lines of pitch counts and the roster system used in Major League Baseball in North America.
- Have bowlers specialise in either Test or one-day cricket.
- Restore the rest day in Test cricket.

More recently, Lillee has acknowledged that his third solution to the problem has become less of a commercial reality in today's world, so he has added another to the list: Ensure injury prevention through core body strengthening exercises. Two of his protégés, Test fast bowlers Brett Lee and Mitchell Johnson, provide great examples of the value of these exercises. They have both overcome lower back problems incurred early in their careers by modifying their bowling actions and including core body stability exercises in their strength and conditioning programs. These exercises have enabled them to better control the position of the trunk to generate powerful movements in the extremities and reduce the strain on the lumbar spine. Some core strengthening exercises are described later in this chapter.

Players also need to be careful when playing on soft grounds because the muscles have to work harder, increasing the risk of soft tissue injuries such as calf and hamstring strains. Alternatively, on hard grounds the likelihood of impact-related injuries to the hip, knee and ankle joints is greater. Alex Kountouris experienced this when he was involved in matches in overseas countries.

> When I was working with the Sri Lankan team preparing to tour England, we trained early in the morning when the grounds were dewy or on the beach sand in trying to replicate English conditions. However, it is always difficult to predict ground conditions. Recently, in South Africa, Australia played on a ground that was as

soft as I had ever seen. The players had to wear football boots to keep a grip on the outer surface. It resulted in four of our players straining their hamstrings. It was our entire quota of hamstring injuries for the year, and we haven't had one since. Other teams had the same problem. There could have been other factors involved, such as it being early in the season and after travelling, but I am convinced that the ground surface was the main factor. We had the same problem with a sand-based ground in Antigua in the West Indies being hard to run across and causing a calf strain.

At the club level of the game, players often encounter rough surfaces, which increase the likelihood of ankle injuries. In these conditions and on damp grounds or wickets, players must choose the right footwear to maintain stability.

Injuries from collisions with boundary fences have been greatly reduced by the compulsory use of boundary ropes, instituted in 2000 after recommendations were made following injury surveillance. Some coaches are reluctant to involve players in the various codes of football to provide variety and cross training because of the fear that their unfamiliarity with the skills involved will increase the risk of injury. However, because players enjoy variety in training, many coaches believe it is a risk worth taking with the right instruction and warm-up beforehand.

TIP Coaches need to be alert to the potential for players to be injured during practice sessions. This means maintaining a close eye on bowlers' workloads, safety in batting and fielding drills and the participation of players in other sporting activities.

Injury Rehabilitation

The rehabilitation program for an injury will depend on the injury and the role of the player. For example, a fast bowler and a cover fielder may both be suffering from hamstring strains. The fast bowler, however, lands on the front leg during the delivery stride and puts all the body weight on the hamstrings, whereas the fielder sprinting from cover to effect a run-out places a smaller load in a shorter time period on these muscles. Their rehabilitation programs should reflect these differences, and the program load should be carefully monitored. Kountouris described how fast bowlers and cover fielders should approach the task.

> With fast bowlers we have them do a lot of single-leg work using their body weight to replicate what is happening during the bowling action, because every time that they land on the front leg, it is with a load 5-6 times body weight. The hamstrings must be able to handle this more than 100 times a day. On the other hand, cover fielders are going to have to sprint fast and hard, so we would have them do a lot more short runs, accelerating and decelerating.

The second consideration with a rehabilitation program is the need to constantly modify the exercises because, as the player recovers, the program will become outdated. Changes in the number of repetitions and sets, and even the exercise itself, will be necessary if the training load is becoming too easy and no longer appropriate.

Physiotherapist **JAMES PYKE** believes that, because cricket is predominantly a throwing sport, the shoulder joint must be both flexible and strong. He has focused on this joint to illustrate the approach that should be taken during the rehabilitation process, as well as indicate some of the specific exercises that can be used to improve shoulder flexibility and strength.

The most important muscles in the shoulder region to require conditioning are the rotator cuff group, which are the primary stabilisers of the shoulder girdle. Pyke lists the following as essential stages in the process of shoulder rehabilitation:

1. Diagnose accurately the severity of the injury for appropriate early management.
2. Settle inflammation and pain (ice, pain relief, anti-inflammatories).
3. Restore flexibility and strength.
4. Throw over short distances.
5. Return gradually to full training.

Keeping an eye on technique during rehabilitation is essential to ensure that the program is not contributing to the injury and inhibiting the rehabilitation process. Hence, the return to training should be done gradually to ensure that the healing process is not hindered. Pyke recommends the following exercises to improve the flexibility of the shoulder joint:

- *Shoulder drop.* Lie on the back with hands clasped behind the head. Pull elbows back and pinch shoulder blades together.
- *Towel stretch.* Hold towel behind the back with one arm over the head and the other near the lower back. Pull the lower arm upwards by lifting the towel (see figure 1.1).

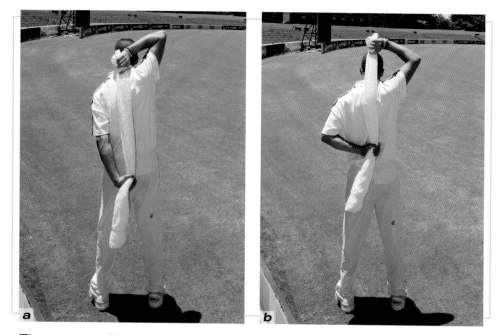

Figure 1.1 Towel stretch.

- *Across body pull.* Gently pull on the elbow with the opposite hand until the hand is on the back of the other shoulder.
- *Corner stretch.* Stand in the corner with hands on each wall at shoulder height. Lean forward until the stretch is felt across the chest.

Following are Pyke's recommended shoulder-strengthening exercises:

- *Wall kiss.* With hands shoulder-width apart, lean forward to the wall squeezing the shoulder blades together and touching the nose on the wall. Commence with two hands on the wall, gradually progressing to one.
- *Resistance tubing.* With tubing secured in a door or fence at shoulder height, pull down across the body as though throwing a ball (see figure 1.2).
- *Plyometrics.* Throw and catch a medicine ball against a wall.
- *Isometric external rotation in adduction.* Move the arm across the midline to a point beyond the opposite shoulder. Resist rotating back by placing the other hand on the back of the working hand at 40 percent of maximum contraction.

Figure 1.2   Resistance tubing exercise.

Exercises that enhance core stability provide muscle control around the torso area where strength and coordination of the abdominal, back and buttock muscles help to stabilise the spine and provide a strong base for movement of the extremities. In short, good core stability lessens the stress on the shoulder joint in throwing and bowling actions. Following are some regularly used core stability exercises:

- *Plank.* Support the body on the elbows and either the knees or toes, keeping the pelvis in a neutral position. Draw in the lower abdominal muscles, keeping the body straight. Hold for 30 seconds; repeat several times (see figure 1.3).

Figure 1.3 Plank.

- *Side plank.* Lie on the side supporting the body on one elbow directly below the shoulder, creating a straight line with the whole body; hold for 30 seconds; repeat on each side several times (see figure 1.4).

Figure 1.4 Side plank.

- *Dead bug.* Lie flat on the back with arms stretched above the head. Bring the knees to the chest. Flatten the back against the floor and slowly lower the left leg to the floor while the left arm follows the leg movement. With the arm and leg close to the floor, hold the position for 10 seconds. Repeat the movement and hold the position on the right side (see figure 1.5).

Figure 1.5 Dead bug.

- *Superman.* Lie on the abdomen with arms fully extended above the head and feet 30 centimetres apart. Inhale deeply and, while exhaling, squeeze the buttocks and raise the trunk, arms and head. Hold the position for 10 seconds. Repeat 10 times (see figure 1.6).

Figure 1.6 Superman.

Illness Prevention

Players must replace fluids regularly to reduce the effects of dehydration during cricket in the summer. Water and sport drinks must be readily available at practice sessions and matches. Hydrating is an individual matter, and the frequency of drinking and the carbohydrate and electrolyte content of the fluid will depend on the degree of heat and humidity and the activity level of the player.

The experience of **DEAN JONES** when he made a historic double century in oppressive conditions in the tied Test match in Madras (Chennai) in 1986 underlines how serious dehydration can become. After vomiting regularly throughout the latter stages of his innings, he finished up in hospital on a saline drip. In his medical report of the Australian team's 2007 tour of India, John Orchard suggested that the severity of Jones' situation may have been averted if intravenous rehydration had been medically administered during a lunch or tea break once a heat illness had been diagnosed.

TIP Players should replace fluid regularly while they are fielding or batting for lengthy periods, especially on hot days. This not only maintains their concentration and performance but also protects them against dehydration and heat illness.

Orchard also recommends that all players and officials be immunised against hepatitis A and B, diphtheria, tetanus, typhoid, cholera and meningococcal disease before embarking on tours to overseas countries. Food poisoning and associated vomiting and diarrhoea are also big issues, particularly on the subcontinent. Personal hygiene is strongly encouraged, and players should be required to wash their hands before eating anything. The medical staff should make sure that all the food is well cooked; it must be over 60 degrees before anyone eats it. They should make the cooks aware of this beforehand. It is also important that players drink only bottled water and cold drinks. This includes water used to brush their teeth.

The medical policy should be that any player who becomes ill with a sore throat or a cold should immediately be quarantined. Unfortunately, players can be contagious before they get any symptoms and can infect teammates in close proximity to them in aircraft, buses and common team rooms. This makes preventing the spread of illness difficult.

It is also important to minimise the effects of jet lag when travelling long distances to other countries. Players should sleep according to the time zone at their intended destination. Upon arrival, they should go into the sunlight as soon as possible to stimulate the release of melatonin, which helps the brain adjust to it being daytime. While on the plane players should wear anti-DVT (deep vein thrombosis) stockings to minimise the risk of getting blood clots. Also, any player with a sore back should avoid sitting in the one place for more than 30 minutes.

Following are guidelines for club players based on the experiences of international players on overseas tours:

- Wash hands before handling food.
- Use separate drink containers.
- Stretch after driving to a match.
- If you are a fast bowler, drink while fielding at fine leg.
- If you are ill, stay away from other members of the team.

Warm-Up and Cool-Down Practices

To optimise preparation for any type of physical activity, the muscles involved should be both warm and well stretched. This ensures that they will function at their best and be less susceptible to injury. By the same token, the cool-down process following exercise should be gradual and complete to enable full recovery for the next training session or contest.

Warm-Up

The prematch warm-up needs to be specific for each player and the match situation, as well as the environmental conditions. As Kountouris states:

> On a warm day players need to concentrate more on stretching than running, whereas on a cold day running helps to raise the body temperature before any involvement with high-impact activities. It is also important to consider what occurred on the previous day of a match. If it was a long day in the field, the warm-up should be low intensity; whereas if the players were sitting around, it would need to be more intense.

In general the warm-up routine should involve some jogging, a combination of passive and dynamic stretching followed by some higher-intensity sprints, more specific stretching (e.g., shoulders, hamstrings) and finally, high-impact, specific activities such as throwing and catching. James Pyke points to the uncertainty of cricket and the difficulty of predicting when a player will be called into action. He provides the following warm-up suggestions for change bowlers and down-the-order batsmen:

> A change bowler may have to wait in the field for an hour or more before being called into the action. Preparation should include regular stretching exercises for the shoulder, trunk and leg muscles as well as rolling the arm over in the pattern of the delivery. Shoulder rotations; forward rotation side bends; back extensions; and quadriceps, hamstring and calf stretches should be done to enable a bowler to bowl a quality first over rather than take one or two overs to get into their stride.
>
> A down-the-order batter is in an even worse predicament while waiting for a wicket to fall. Preparation could include fast-foot reaction drills using the agility ladder, half-pitch throw-downs and shortened run-a-threes, repeated every 15 minutes to heighten mental alertness. In the future, preparation may also include actual footwork drills against computer-generated virtual reality.

Cool-Down

Generally, recovery is assisted by a cool-down period that includes walking and stretching at the end of a training session or after a match in which the player has spent a lengthy period in the field. For best results, this should be accompanied by rehydration and, ideally, cold water therapy, massage or both. This process can last up to an hour and include a debrief from the coach and the captain. Recent research is providing a stronger physiological basis for cold water therapy to match the psychological and team building benefits of players spending time together in baths and pools. In some sports the process is repeated on the morning after a match. This practice should be considered for bowlers after long spells, for batters who have played long innings and for the entire team when it has spent a day in the field.

Summary

This chapter covers the principles and methods underlying the physical preparation of players as well as the common injuries and illnesses they experience. It draws on the fields of sport science and sports medicine and highlights what players should be doing to enhance their performance, as well as how cricket-related injuries and illnesses can be prevented and, if they do occur, what steps should be taken to ensure recovery. Following are some of the key points from the chapter:

- Ultimately, training should meet the specific demands of the game and the specific needs of each player.
- Progressively increasing the training load must be balanced by giving sufficient time and attention to recovery.
- Injuries have become more common as a result of the increased workload of busy national and international playing schedules.
- Fast bowlers are most likely to be injured, particularly with side and groin strains and ankle impingement injuries.
- The intensity of Twenty20 cricket has increased injuries among batters and fielders, notably shoulder, hamstring and calf strains.
- Workloads should be carefully monitored throughout the season, particularly among fast bowlers.
- Player safety should be given high priority when fielding on different ground surfaces and in the proximity of boundary fences, as well as during participation in other sporting activities.
- Injury rehabilitation programs should be individualised depending on the specific nature of the injury and the role of the player, and monitored closely throughout the recovery period.
- Immunisation against infectious diseases should occur before visiting overseas countries, particularly those on the subcontinent.
- Players should give the highest priority to personal hygiene at all times when travelling.
- On hot days players need to pay particular attention to regularly replacing the fluid lost in sweating. This is best done using bottled sport drinks that contain low concentrations of carbohydrate and electrolytes.

- Warm-up routines need to be specific for each player and allow for the uncertainty associated with their involvement in the match.
- A cool-down period at the end of training or an intensive period of a match should include walking; stretching; rehydration; and cold water therapy, massage or both.

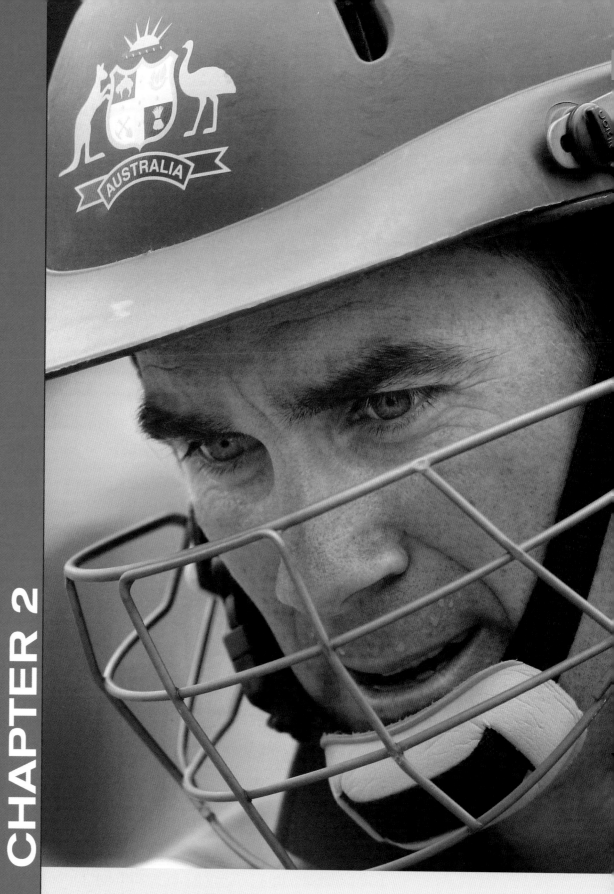

CHAPTER 2

Mental
Preparation

Cricket is a tough mental game and involves many opportunities for players to experience a plethora of emotions. These can range from the unbridled joy experienced when a blistering cover drive pierces the field to bring up a century, to the devastation experienced when the stumps are shattered by the first delivery faced.

When we reflect on some of the nuances of the game, the difficulty dealing with the mental challenges cricket provides becomes clear. Consider the following aspects of the game to which players have to adapt:

- Apart from the opening batters and bowlers, essentially all other participants don't know exactly when they are going to be involved in the match. Such uncertainty can play havoc with their preparation. Frequently, players are ready to go at the start of play but don't feature in the match until four hours later when they may have become listless or distracted.

- Once a wicket falls, a batter has only two minutes to be ready to face the first delivery. Typically, this means facing a group of 11 opponents who are confident and aggressive because they have just gained a wicket.

- There is no opportunity to practice on the pitch prior to the match. In other sports such as football, hockey, baseball and tennis, players can become accustomed to the conditions before they compete. Clearly, then, cricketers face more uncertainty as they prepare for their involvement.

- A batter may bat for only one minute in a day of batting. That is, the batter can be out first ball and have to sit and watch 599 balls for the rest of the day. Surely there can be no worse torture for a serious athlete who has prepared diligently than to have the event be over in an instant. For this reason, players find it difficult to take risks and often adopt less attacking styles of play.

- The length of the match creates a mental as well as physical challenge. Fielders can essentially play no part in the match for hours on end and then suddenly be expected to dive and catch a nick from a batter flying at great speed in their vicinity.

- The fate of batters is largely under their control, but in some cases an umpire error can lead to a premature exit from the ground. Bowlers too can suffer frustration from umpires who fail to detect an obvious nick to the wicketkeeper. Players need to learn to be prepared for such disappointment and focus on their next task.

- Bowlers must often rely on others to bring them success. For instance, a batter can be lured into playing a false shot, but the ball must be caught for a bowler's plan to be realised. Dealing with the disappointment of a dropped catch can be difficult for bowlers because the outcome is essentially out of their control.

These points illustrate just some of the mental challenges cricketers face regularly. This chapter explores ways of developing mental skills to enhance performance consistency. Each of the chapters on cricket skills (chapters 3 through 6) address specific practices that players adopt to enhance their mental skills. The purpose here is to present some strategies and practices that have been identified by mental skills practitioners who have worked with professional cricket teams.

In 1992, Graham Winter, a former first-class cricketer for South Australia, published an outstanding book titled *The Psychology of Cricket*; many of the practices outlined here have been gleaned from that book. More recently, at the University of Western Australia, Dr. **DANIEL GUCCIARDI** and Dr. **SANDY GORDON** have researched mental toughness in cricket, and **MARTIN TOBIN** has created some cricket-specific practical activities to consolidate players' mental skills, which have also been included. Additionally, one of authors of this book, Ken Davis, has worked extensively in sport psychology in cricket, and some of his ideas and practices have been included in this chapter. Professor **BRUCE ABERNETHY** has researched widely how elite athletes develop anticipation skills to give themselves more time to make decisions and respond. His thoughts on ways of honing anticipation skills are extremely relevant to coaches and aspiring cricketers. These are presented towards the end of this chapter.

Mental Toughness

History is replete with examples of successful outcomes that have been achieved by players with inferior talent and fitness than their opponents. Tennis aficionados would recall how Arthur Ashe at age 31 dismantled the game of the seemingly invincible reigning champion Jimmy Connors in the 1975 Wimbledon tennis final. In the 1980 Olympics, an ice hockey team of amateur and collegiate players from the USA surprised everyone by beating the highly fancied and more professional team from the Soviet Union, in what has become known as the Miracle on Ice. Greece won the 2004 Euro Soccer championships when ranked 200/1 outsiders. In 2005, cricket minnows Bangladesh pulled off what was probably the biggest shock in the history of cricket when they beat the world champion Aussies in a one-day match. The Australian team had been 100/1 on to win before the match.

Clearly, these teams or individuals did not suddenly produce more skill or fitness, so the keys to these upsets had to involve matters of the mind. The winners possessed superior mind strength on the day of the match. Because these mental skills can be taught, the development of mental toughness in cricketers should become a major part in any elite program. Typically, mental toughness has been achieved through trial and error. Often, however, players do not find the keys to mental toughness and are either lost to the sport or are continually failing to live up to the expectations that their talent may presume. Mind control comes through practice and perseverance. Once achieved, it is like swimming with the tide. Conversely, many players are constantly swimming against the current and never realise their potential.

It behooves all those entrusted with preparing cricketers for competition to not only understand what mental toughness is, but also to know how best to accelerate its progress in players striving for better performance. Most people have had some experience with mental toughness in their lives. All of us could give examples of mentally tough athletes and could, if pressed, identify some behaviours that illustrate this trait. We can readily observe these traits in our normal lives. We see people who recover from adversity, who persevere with every task they are set and who are able to deal with any situation they meet with a positive mindset. These traits and many more are clearly observable in the cauldron in which elite athletes are often immersed.

Some people have researched mental toughness trying to find a definitive set of behaviours; this research provides a useful starting point for any investigation of this complex topic. However, the search for ways to enhance mental toughness should not be limited by formal research. It should be a never ending process and continue to involve the close examination of athletes under the pressure of intense competition.

After researching several sports, Gucciardi and Gordon identified the following core characteristics in the make-up of a mentally tough performer. These qualities form the basis of their inventory of mental toughness, which is available through Cricket Australia.

- *Self-belief*—A belief or confidence in one's own physical and mental ability.
- *Personal values*—Values and beliefs that are relevant to becoming a better person and athlete through the sporting experience.
- *Self-motivation*—An intrinsic motivation or desire for competitive challenges as well as to work hard to achieve individual or team success.
- *Positive and tough attitude*—Maintaining a positive and tough attitude when confronted with positive and negative pressure, adversity or challenge.
- *Thriving through pressure*—The ability to execute skills and procedures under pressure and accepting pressure as a necessary aspect of becoming a better person and athlete.
- *Resilience*—The ability to adapt and bounce back from adversity or challenge.
- *Attentional control*—The ability to focus attention on aspects relevant to one's performance.
- *Affective intelligence*—The ability to manage emotions, feelings or mood to optimise performance.
- *Game awareness*—Knowledge of the processes of a sport and one's ability to execute such processes.

Most people would accept that all of the preceding qualities are relevant to the continuing process of uncovering the specifics of mental toughness. However, it is reasonable to assume that each person reading this book could add to the list in a meaningful manner. Following are some additional attributes to consider. These have been gleaned from both our own personal experience and discussions with athletes and coaches.

- A sense of *pride* underpins most mentally tough people and can motivate them to remain focused on their performance no matter what adversity they may be facing. Such people's self-worth is closely linked to their performance, and so they are driven to put forward their maximum effort and thought at all times.

- Mentally tough people *take responsibility for their actions*. When evaluating their performance, they look first at themselves and determine how they can best improve. They seldom blame others for poor performance and can quickly look forward to preparing for their next contest. They learn lessons from every contest.

- *Mental and physical courage* can play a significant part in developing consistently tough performances. In cricket it takes considerable courage to get in behind a fast bowler hurling a thunderbolt into the rib cage.

- Most athletes develop specific match plans that either suit their skill set or meet the needs of the team. However, mentally tough athletes seem to be able to *adapt* their plans when they are not working. This requires both stoicism to keep plugging away at a match plan and adaptability.

- A good gauge of mental toughness is how well players *react to the hard things* in their preparation and match performance. Most people find it easy to do things they enjoy. However, those who can commit to doing all the difficult or challenging things in sport with maximum intensity are well on the way to achieving mental toughness. In cricket these hard things include the following:
  - Working on turns to improve running between wickets
  - A batter running as hard for their partner's runs as their own
  - In the field, moving to back up and being involved for every ball that is hit
  - Consistently stretching one's body to maintain flexibility
  - Jogging into fielding positions between overs even in stifling heat
  - Maintaining bowling speed even when fatigued
  - Training on skills or fitness alone, away from the club environment
  - Working consistently to improve a weakness
  - Putting as much effort into fitness work as skill practice
  - Training hard and with purpose even when stressed in other aspects of life

- Probably the best indicator of mental toughness is a player's level of *consistency*. Consistent performers are able to overcome adversity, poor preparation, excess fatigue and other life stressors to perform close to their best every day. They may not always succeed, but rest assured, they will be always be giving maximum effort and thought to their performances.

- In these times of player empowerment it has become a common practice for players to provide honest feedback to each other about matters on and off field that affect their performance. An *ability to accept criticism* without taking it personally and dwelling on it takes a lot of mental strength. Tough people see this process as part of the continuing quest for excellence and profit by the advice.

TIP The best players display mental toughness in the way they approach practice and their performance in matches. Coaches need to be aware of these behaviours and positively reinforce members of the squad who display them.

Now that we have gained some insight into the qualities of mentally tough cricketers, we will explore ways of developing mental skills to ensure that players possess the hardness and strength of mind needed for handling any situation.

Mental Skills Practices

The following practices can be done either on or off the field. Initially, it is important to consider the type of game for which a player is preparing. The Twenty20 format requires a different mindset than 50-over matches, which, in turn, are vastly different from matches lasting in excess of two days. Practices need to be structured to cater to the style of matches. For instance, leaving the ball alone for a batter may be appropriate in longer versions of the game and should be practiced. However, in preparing for Twenty20 matches, it is not desirable to spend much practice time letting the ball pass through to the wicketkeeper.

As mentioned earlier, throughout his book *The Psychology of Cricket*, Graham Winter outlines many activities for practicing mental skills. These are presented in summary form here, along with some practices adopted by Ken Davis. These practices can comfortably be used to enhance the mental skills of cricketers.

General Mental Skills

The following practices can be used to improve the mental skills of players in all areas of the game. They should be applied during training routines as a prelude to being used to enhance performance in competition matches.

FINDING THE RIGHT FEELING STATE

For players with a passive attitude before a match, an energetic warm-up with forceful instructions is recommended to raise aggression levels. The coach in this situation would consistently use a strong voice to encourage the players to increase the tempo of their preparation. Conversely, with players who are overly excited before a match, it might be necessary to do some relaxation exercises to calm them down before the contest. Deep breathing and listening to calming music or hearing positive reinforcement are some useful strategies to settle this type of player.

REINFORCING CORRECT MOVEMENT PATTERNS

Because reinforcing correct movement patterns is important for confidence in developing automatic skill responses, coaches should encourage players to repeat successful drills. In practice, when players perform a drill well, they should repeat it for several days in a row. Alternatively, if they are having difficulty with their skills during a particular session, the coach should try to finish on a note where the players achieve some success.

VISUALISING SKILLED MOVEMENT PATTERNS

Players should visualise the way they want to perform a skill. For example, with catching, players should picture themselves between deliveries running to take a catch and should strive to remember the feelings of how the ball is to be taken in the hands. Visualisation can also help bowlers as they prepare to bowl. A bowler should see and feel the delivery she wants to bowl; then execute it in a relaxed manner. Visualising is different for batters because they do not know where the ball is going to be bowled. However, visualisation can still be useful for developing the feelings and rhythms of particular shots.

ENHANCING CONSISTENCY

Players in every position should spend time establishing and maintaining the routines they do before each delivery to make sure they do not just drift into a delivery without appropriate focus and care. Routines are very individual, but they should be done consistently. For example, a batter between deliveries might walk down the pitch and sweep away any bits of loose turf; then turn around, take a deep breath and relax the shoulders before moving into a batting stance in a systematic way. He might want to control his thought process by focusing on a swing thought (such as 'play straight', 'quick feet' or 'be aggressive') when facing the next delivery. Bowlers, fielders and wicketkeepers should adopt a similar process. Practicing these routines should become a part of training sessions so that, like all other skills, they become automatic and set the player in a state of readiness for each delivery in a match.

MODELLING ELITE PERFORMERS

Modelling the smoothly coordinated movement of a player can be done by watching the performance repeatedly on a television screen. Ideally, the player should become absorbed in the movement and try to feel the rhythm exhibited by the skilled performer. This process has commercially been known as sybervision and relies on a process known as neurolinguistic programming to cement the skill into the subconscious of the athlete. When we consider how easy it is for some young people to mimic the actions of star players, the value of such an exercise is apparent. A player may achieve the same outcome by watching himself repeatedly doing a skill well.

CONTROLLING SELF-TALK

Controlling self-talk is vital in cricket. Often, players' thoughts are negative, which can inhibit their performance. To control self-talk, a player must first make herself aware of their negative thoughts and find ways to stop them immediately. For example, some athletes visualise a stop sign in their minds. Others may simply say 'Stop' to themselves whenever negative thoughts occur. The aim is to counter a negative thought with an appropriate positive one. For batters and wicketkeepers, the focus should return to the ball, and their thoughts should be positive and energising. Such thoughts as 'Be positive with my feet' or 'In behind the ball' may be appropriate for a batter; a keeper's thought may be 'Watch the ball into my gloves'. Bowlers may think only of the feeling or rhythm they feel when they bowl well. When positive thoughts are going through the mind, it is not possible to have negative thoughts. This skill does take practice, but it can be done in all aspects of one's life. Training oneself to see the positives in every situation will soon result in positive self-talk pervading one's internal dialogue.

CONTROLLING THE CONTROLLABLES

Players should learn to focus on things that are under their control. So often, players are distracted by such things as crowd noise, pitch conditions, fielders dropping catches, umpiring decisions and sledging from an opponent. These are all aspects of the match that are clearly out of their control and should not be allowed to enter the mind. Refocusing on the essentials of the task and executing the skills precisely is crucial here. For example, when an umpiring decision goes against a bowler, the bowler must get involved immediately with planning and executing the next delivery with energy and controlled aggression. Dwelling on the past misfortune can distract bowlers and reduce their intensity. So often at training, players curse when batting under adverse conditions and then reduce their focus by playing wild shots during the remaining part of their batting time. Such players need to accept the conditions and challenge themselves to cope, because there will come a day when match conditions are not ideal. When that happens, such practice may be beneficial.

One way to improve the ability to handle distractions is to practice with them present. Coaches can have players talk to the batter or walk behind the bowler's arm to simulate possible match situations. So long as these activities do not threaten the safety of participants, they can become fun interludes in training sessions.

Restoring Confidence

Confidence is one of those curious states that can come and go very quickly. Fundamentally, one needs a strong belief that the task at hand is achievable. Doubts, however, can hover around even the most confident person. A series of poor performances, a pitch that is producing uncertain bounce, a menacing bowler or even an ailing body can erode a batter's confidence. A bowler may just not feel right in his action, which may produce some errant deliveries, or he may be attacked by a batter, which lessens his confidence. To restore confidence, players should take the following steps:

1. Recall and imagine yourself doing the skills well.
2. Project a positive, calm and composed image at all times.
3. Act confidently as you go out to perform. Use your voice in a strong, authoritative way.
4. Deal with one ball at a time and avoid focusing on past or future events.
5. Focus on the fundamentals of the skills and do not get tied up with too many fancy shots or deliveries.
6. Commit to giving your best effort every ball.
7. Tell yourself you are only one match away from being in good form.
8. Identify the positives in every performance even if they are sometimes difficult to see.
9. Focus on one or two key areas for improvement rather than being overwhelmed with negatives in your performance.
10. Make sure you prepare well for the next contest. Leave training feeling better about your game.

TIP Players must always try to focus on the positive. This means feeling confident about their preparation for the match and being able to deal with any situation that arises while retaining a focus on what is happening presently.

DEALING WITH MISTAKES

In addition to having a routine to precede every delivery, players should have a specific process to deal with mistakes when they occur. Whenever they make mistakes, players should be conditioned to respond in a positive manner. For instance, if a bowler is hit for a six, then she must project a positive and determined image to the batter with no swearing, shaking the head or kicking the ground. As bowlers walk back to their mark, they should analyse what went wrong previously and then dismiss the ball from their minds. They should then focus on the upcoming ball and turn at the top of their mark presenting a strong, aggressive image to the batter. Batters, fielders and wicketkeepers alike should adopt a similar approach to their own errors. This process should be practiced at training and in matches so that it becomes an automatic response.

COPING WITH THE UNEXPECTED

Contingency planning involves thinking of possible scenarios and considering how one might respond. For instance, batters may ask themselves, 'What if a team suddenly adopts a strategy of bowling to a field with six on the leg side?' or, 'What if I am competing against a more highly credentialed opponent?' A coach can throw these situations at the players at regular intervals either in on-field match scenarios or at team meetings. The players themselves can also brainstorm about 'what ifs' and outline strategies for dealing with them. This exercise conditions players to confront difficult situations in their minds so they are better prepared when they occur in matches.

Mental Skills for Batters

Although most of the preceding practices have relevance to batters, some more specific situations need their attention so they can perform consistently at their best.

PRACTICING UNDER ADVERSE CONDITIONS

As mentioned briefly before, players should always bat when difficult pitch conditions occur at training so they are prepared to do so in a match. Some players decline a hit when the ball is moving around off the seam, spinning prodigiously or bouncing either lower or higher than on a true pitch surface because they don't want to lose confidence. Given the potential to lose confidence, it is best then to follow a difficult net session with some confidence-building throw-downs or work with a ball machine.

In addition, if a batter is going through a period in which he is getting out early in an innings, a coach could structure practices so that he has many short hits (say, of less than five minutes) so he can practice the start of the innings many times. This will enhance the batter's performance in matches when commencing an innings.

BUILDING COURAGE FOR FACING PACE BOWLING

Although getting behind the ball when facing express bowling clearly takes courage, it is a sensitive issue with players. No one likes to have a ball projected at speed at her body, but it is important to not let this threat interfere with the fundamental skill of getting one's eyes in line with the ball. Coaches need to explain to players that if they don't look as though they have courage, they will be bombarded with short deliveries for the rest of their careers. They should also point out that everyone fears getting hit with the ball.

Having discussed these practices with players, the coach's next step is to prepare them to play a short ball effectively. The first activity involves facing a tennis ball, preferably on a wooden surface to promote a fast bounce. The tennis ball can be projected from a bowling machine or hit with a tennis racquet with a serving motion. With a softer ball, players have more confidence in getting their bodies in line with the ball. They should still bat with full protective gear and should practice evasion techniques and defensive and aggressive shots.

Once the players have mastered batting to short-pitched bowling with the tennis ball, the coach can introduce harder balls. Golf balls can generate a lot of bounce. Ultimately, players should be able to handle bouncers bowled at pace with a new cricket ball. Coaches should remember that everyone looks a little awkward at some time; however, they should encourage correct positioning (batters getting in line with the ball). Also, because players will inevitably be struck when developing these techniques, they must be prepared for some pain and their courage to get behind the ball must dominate their fear of getting hurt.

Mental Skills for Fielders and Wicketkeepers

The following are mental skill practices that coaches can use with players to improve fielding and wicketkeeping skills in cricket.

SWITCHING FOCUS

When fielding, players can practice switching on their focus at a certain stage of a bowler's run up and switching off their focus when their role in that delivery has clearly passed. For instance, a fielder might zero in on the batter's feet or the edge of the bat. Ideally, fielders should also go through a similar process at practice.

PRACTICING RANDOM CATCHING

Because a player may get to attempt only one or two catches in a day of fielding, it is good practice for a coach to call players out of regular practice to catch a high ball and then return to net practice. Such an activity permits players to practice sporadic catching interspersed with the bowling, ground fielding and moving to position that occur in a match.

Wicketkeepers also need to develop similar routines to ready themselves for action. In their case, an obvious practice is to cue in on the ball during the bowler's approach. As well as doing a lot of continuous catching practice to fine tune skills, they should also practice catching intermittently as they would in a match.

Mental Skills for Bowlers

Bowling is the only closed skill in cricket because its action is not dependent on anyone else. Bowlers determine when they will start their approach and when they will let go of the ball. They do not have to prepare for any of the uncertainty that surrounds all other skills in the game. As a consequence, from a mental viewpoint, bowling is a much simpler process than other skills in the game. Coaches can use the following practices to improve the mental skills of bowlers.

RELIVING EXPERIENCES OF SUCCESS

An effective way to increase accuracy in bowling is to practice bowling to a spot on the pitch. When the bowler is successful in hitting that spot, she should think about the feeling of that delivery. Then, she should try to repeat the feeling without worrying about direction.

Further Mental Practices Identified by Sport Scientists

Sport scientists have recently begun to investigate the area of mental practice in cricket. Daniel Gucciardi and Sandy Gordon, mentioned previously, identified the following strategies and techniques to facilitate the development of mental toughness:

- Expose players to a variety of experiences, pressures and adversities including failure.
- Encourage players to take responsibility for their actions.
- Simulate competition pressures during training.
- Focus on a player's strengths while emphasising weaknesses as areas for improvement.
- Provide positive reinforcement and encouragement at all times.
- Have key people model mentally tough values, attitudes, emotions and thoughts.
- Constantly challenge players.
- Encourage discussion and debate so that players have an outlet to voice their opinions and, in some cases, their frustrations.
- Self-reflect on critical incidents both within and outside the game.

The latter point warrants further comment. Although it is important to involve the players in discussions, they need to understand that, ultimately, the coach will have to make some decisions and these may not always align with the thoughts of all players. Once he has expressed an opinion, the mentally tough player gets on with things even if the coach has not adopted his suggestion.

FINDING THE IDEAL PERFORMANCE STATE

Essentially, bowlers need to recreate the feeling state that coincides with their best performances as often as they can. Being aware of tension levels in their hands and shoulders is a good way to identify this ideal performance state. Once bowlers have identified this state, they need to be able to either relax key areas of their body, or in some cases (such as in excessive heat) become more energised. A bowler may walk back from an errant delivery shaking the bowling hand loosely at the side to release the tension felt in the delivery. Deep breathing can also assist in lowering tension levels. When the situation requires more energy and excitement, the player should do anything to get the body operating with zest. Running on the spot, building up a dislike of particular batters, thinking of one's own goals and focusing on the importance of the match to the team are all useful strategies for becoming more aroused.

Mental Skills Training on the Field

With the gradual acceptance of sport psychologists as part of the preparation of elite teams, these consultants have begun to do some work on the field within the normal training session. Thus, mental training can be integrated with fitness and skill development. Typically, at club level mental training occurs almost by accident rather than systematically.

It is refreshing and timely that these professionals are now addressing the need to develop practical on-field solutions to mental problems in cricket. Sport psychology graduate, teacher, and head coach at the University Cricket Club in Western Australia, Martin Tobin, is one such professional. Tobin has produced an impressive nine-session format of activities that teach effective mind control in cricket. Tobin covers the following topics, many of which have been outlined previously:

- Setting goals for training
- Starting an innings
- Shadow batting, which involves practicing the skill without a ball
- The art of watching the ball
- Batting pre-delivery routine
- Spin bowling focus
- Cricket attitude moments such as playing and missing and being dropped from the team
- Thought control
- Dealing with errors

These practical sessions provide the opportunity to practice the mental skills of goal setting, imagery (visualisation), concentration, self-confidence and positive self-talk. They are geared towards three levels: introductory, intermediate and advanced. Two examples, one for the introductory level and one for the advanced level, are provided here.

INTRODUCTORY ACTIVITY: THE ART OF WATCHING THE BALL

The objective of this activity is to develop batters' selective attention skills by developing a visual tracking strategy for focusing on the point of release of the ball from the bowler's hand.

1. Have players stand behind a batter in a net and observe the bowler running in and delivering the ball. The focus should be on the point of release of the ball and then on the seam of the ball as it approaches the batter. Players are instructed to 'find the ball'.

2. Two players are engaged, with one batting and the other throwing the ball to the batter. The batter takes up a ready position with eyes closed. On the command 'Now', which is made just prior to the feeder's release, the batter opens his eyes and makes a stroke. Reducing the time to 'find the ball' overloads the visual system and trains players to find the point of release. Note that this drill can be used with a bowling machine with the 'Now' command corresponding to the ball being placed into the machine. Tennis balls can be used to reduce the chance of injury and because they can be released at higher speeds. Batters are encouraged to use the 'Now' command as a verbal trigger for peak concentration at the point of release whenever they are batting at practice or in a match.

3. The visual system can be overloaded in another drill that requires the players to receive a number of deliveries in quick succession. The time between deliveries allows the batter to regain her stance only after the previous stroke, and to refocus on the anticipated point of release.

ADVANCED ACTIVITY: CONCENTRATING WHEN SPIN BOWLING

The objective of this activity is to refine the concentration skills of spin bowlers through fostering bowler/coach discussions.

1. Have the bowler complete an over without a batter present using a normal match routine. Then have the bowler bowl further overs that require fielding from self-bowling, or when a batter is present, ask the bowler to define the most critical concentration moment (e.g., top of the mark, point of release).

2. Evaluate the bowler's performance after bowling another over while nominating the type of delivery at the top of the mark. Follow up by questioning the bowler about the effectiveness of this strategy before bowling a further over to evaluate concentration and performance.

3. Ask the bowler what mental triggers (thoughts, images), verbal triggers (self-talk) and physical triggers (grip, wrist position) she is using to produce peak concentration. Evaluate the bowler's performance after bowling overs with different concentration triggers.

Any coach can use Tobin's approach. Essentially, it involves considering important mental skills in cricket and then devising activities that allow the players to learn the techniques in a practical setting. These activities should not be too time-consuming because the concentration spans of many athletes on such activities may not match the coach's expectations. The challenge is to motivate the players over time by showing them the relevance of the activities in improving performance. A useful strategy is to explain how other high-level performers have benefited from such activities.

The development of the mental skills is important to producing a positive mindset. However, much of these skills lose their benefit if the player is unable to move into position quickly enough to execute the physical skills in an unhurried, smooth manner. High-level performers use cues to anticipate what is about to happen so they can position themselves early to execute their skills.

Developing Anticipation Skills

One of the characteristics of great players is that they never appear hurried when executing skills. This is the case with top batters, even against fast bowlers, and with wicketkeepers and fielders who always seem to get into the correct position early. High-speed film of these players confirms that they move early into stable body and head positions, which is essential for skilful batting and catching.

How are they able to do this? Professor Bruce Abernethy from the University of Queensland, and a former first-grade cricketer himself, has led the way in Australia in studying anticipation in fast ball sports. Acknowledging that a batter has insufficient time to make a decision after the ball has been released from a fast bowler's hand, he looked for other answers. He found that batters acquire knowledge of a bowler's favoured line and length and sequence of deliveries in particular circumstances. For example, ball-by-ball statistics enable them to learn more about bowlers' preferred options and sequences. He also found that batters can observe elements of the bowler's approach and delivery action before the ball is released and learn to predict the type and length of the ball about to be bowled. This learning process requires the use of video technology. Abernethy explained:

> One way involves filming the bowler from the batter's normal stance position and then editing the collected video so that the display goes blank (is occluded) at or before the ball is released. The batter's task, when viewing such video, is to either select the type and length of the delivery (from a limited range of options) or alternatively to shadow bat (as if he were actually facing the bowler shown on the video). An alternative, more technologically challenging method is to have batsmen wear special liquid crystal goggles that can be turned from transparent to opaque on command. With this method players attempt to bat as they would normally while facing bowlers delivering a softer than usual ball. Their vision is occluded at different times before

the ball is actually released. The interest, in this case, is to see whether the batsmen can make contact with the ball or, at least, make the correct critical foot movement decisions in the absence of ball flight information.

Both methods demonstrate that the more highly skilled batters pick up movement pattern information earlier and predict the type and length of the delivery more accurately than those who are less skilled. The most critical information comes from the bowling hand and its relationship to the bowling arm after front foot contact has occurred. Abernethy is of the view that anticipatory skill develops slowly and requires extensive exposure to adult movement patterns.

Retrospective studies of successful batsmen frequently reveal that these players have experienced large amounts of unstructured practice during their developing years (especially informal activities such as backyard cricket) and have had early exposure to playing against adults. The latter may be important not only in providing early opportunities to start learning the features of adult bowling patterns but also in creating situations in which success depends on strategy development. This cannot be achieved, as it may be in junior competition, simply on the basis of physical strength and maturity. Abernethy provided the following list of implications of these findings for practice by batters, bowlers, wicketkeepers and fielders.

Batters

1. At the adult level, the ability to anticipate is a significant predictor of success and needs to be systematically trained.

2. Drills to enhance anticipation need to be introduced into routine practice from an early age.

3. Many conventional practice drills for batting (especially those involving the use of bowling machines) do not train anticipation because the bowler's movement pattern is removed as a component of the drill.

4. Accumulating knowledge about the opposing bowlers can aid successful anticipation.

5. The inclusion of net-based or video-based training in which only prerelease information is available should be considered. This requires batters to make batting responses exclusively on the basis of information from the bowler's run-up and delivery action.

Bowlers

1. It is important for bowlers to maximise the uncertainty they can create for batters and to develop disguise or deception within their delivery actions. This limits batters' early detection of changes in delivery types and delays the decision-making process.

2. Bowlers should obtain objective statistics about their own bowling lines, lengths and sequences; be aware of any predictable patterns that exist; and be prepared to vary them to create uncertainty in batters.

3. Bowlers should systematically practice and refine their skills in holding back critical cues as late as possible and presenting misleading ones. Practice in being able to do this is facilitated by the use of video technology (more information can be found in chapter 10, beginning on page 147).

Wicketkeepers

1. It is obviously advantageous, particularly with spin bowling, for the wicketkeeper to know as early as possible the type of delivery about to be bowled.

2. Although much of the learning required to 'pick' the bowler's delivery may be achieved through repetitive keeping to the bowler in practice sessions, benefits may also be derived from using training regimes similar to those suggested for batsmen.

3. Bowlers can also give a signal to a wicketkeeper to pre-empt a change in delivery, without the batter being aware of it.

Fielders

1. Fielders in key positions such as cover and mid wicket are more likely to be able to intercept the batter's scoring strokes if they can commence their interceptive movements early. This requires being able to anticipate the shot based on the batter's preferred selection or preliminary movements prior to striking the ball.

2. Systematically acquiring knowledge about each batter's preferred strokes plus contextual knowledge about the state of the wicket and the match can help develop accurate expectations about likely events, which will facilitate anticipation.

3. Systematically training the ability to predict shot direction and force from the batter's pre-contact movement, using methods such as video-based practice, may also be beneficial.

4. Conventional fielding drills that simply involve the coach hitting the ball to either side of the fielder do not train anticipation because the batter's precontact movements are removed as a component of the drill.

Abernethy advises that enhancing anticipatory skills effectively takes many years of practice. Anticipation skill training should therefore be built into the practice regimes within developmental programs and not left until adult training. Players and coaches need to be realistic about what improvements can be expected and attained from only short periods of training.

 Being able to anticipate the speed and direction of the ball being bowled is critical for batters and wicketkeepers. Picking up cues from bowlers about to deliver the ball is essential in this process, but it takes time to learn and should be practiced from an early age.

Summary

Cricket is a mentally challenging sport. Developing mental toughness must be an important part of any program dedicated to producing high-quality players. The attributes of mentally tough players explored in this chapter include being self-motivated and self-confident and being able to respond to challenging high-pressure situations and adversity in a positive and focused manner. This requires a strong sense of self-belief and pride in one's performance. Providing positive reinforcement when these behaviours are displayed is an important part of the individual and team development process.

A number of mental skill practices being used in modern cricket to improve match performance are also outlined in the chapter. These are relevant to all types of players and include the following:

- Finding the right feeling state
- Reinforcing correct movement patterns
- Visualising skilled movement patterns
- Enhancing consistency
- Modelling elite performers
- Controlling self-talk
- Controlling the controllables
- Tuning out distractions
- Restoring confidence
- Dealing with mistakes
- Coping with the unexpected

Also included are several specific practices for batters, bowlers, fielders and wicketkeepers to improve their anticipation and concentration skills, their courage and their ability to perform under adverse conditions. These are presented as part of the process of fostering coach–player discussions.

Game Skill Development

The emergence of the Twenty20 format makes a clear statement to players. They must have a versatile skill set to make their mark in the modern game. No longer can a player just be a slow-scoring batter or a pace bowler or a specialist slips fielder. When the occasion demands, in either the short or long form of the game, the player needs to be able to adapt to the situation by, for example, batting aggressively and scoring quickly, bowling a tight line and length or covering the ground quickly while patrolling the mid wicket boundary line.

Part II contains a number of practices that are designed to enhance the performance of batters, bowlers, fielders and wicketkeepers. Several of them have been provided by some of the best male and female exponents of these skills to have ever graced our cricket fields. Others have come from coaches who have had a significant impact on player and team performance at the highest level of cricket. Collectively, these people have contributed some unique cricket training formats to meet the demands of the modern game.

Chapter 3 encourages batters to study the best players in action; to divide their practice time in the nets into the segments of an innings; and to use throw-downs, ball drops and ball machines to improve specific aspects of their technique. Examples of team batting strategies and successful batting partnerships are also given.

The approach and delivery action of pace bowlers is given considerable attention in chapter 4. The purpose of this is to reduce the number of no balls bowled as well as the chance of injury, particularly to the lower back region.

Spinners bowl over bars or hurdles and at targets to improve the trajectory and accuracy of their deliveries. All bowlers are encouraged to operate with a plan in mind, based on their evaluation of a batter either from previous experience or from video footage.

Modern fielders must be multi-skilled and able to catch, ground field and throw irrespective of the position they are occupying in the field. Chapter 5 provides a number of competitive practice drills involving small groups to better mirror match intensity. A central figure in the fielding team who needs to participate in these drills is the wicketkeeper, who must not only have good catching and stumping skills but also maintain team enthusiasm. This is addressed in chapter 6. Chapter 7 describes a number of practice formats for batters and bowlers based on the principles of skill and fitness training. These are aimed at maximising participation, providing variety and maintaining pressure while still giving a high priority to the health and safety of the players.

CHAPTER 3

Batting

Batting provides a unique sporting challenge for those who play cricket. On some occasions batters can ply their craft for only one delivery, and then be left to watch the remainder of the day from the stands. A batting error can produce the most severe of outcomes; it is akin to a soccer player being sent off the field straight after the kick-off.

Of course, in cricket, batting errors do not always result in dismissals, but because they can, batters are under extreme pressure. The will to survive often dominates the desire to score, which can result in very slow play. Practice for batting must balance the need to survive with the ability to score runs as quickly as possible. Traditional net practice at the club level typically has allowed about 10 to 15 minutes of batting, which hardly replicates the mental and physical requirements of batting in a match for long periods when scoring a century.

Serious batters have long identified the inadequacy of this team practice approach to their preparation and have engaged others to give them a succession of throw-downs or, more recently, have used ball machines to increase their batting workload. However, because these approaches still don't simulate match conditions, batters have had to be resourceful in using their practice time efficiently. Some of these ideas for more effective practice to prepare batters for competition are presented in this chapter.

Batting Skills and Strategies

Several players modelled their techniques and strategies on particular players or found a mentor to guide them in developing their game. Dean Jones said he loved the way former Test player Julian Wiener hit balls straight in practice so he would not hit the side net when he batted. **IAN REDPATH** used John Shaw (ex Victorian player) as a mentor at South Melbourne when he first went to the club:

> John Shaw was a great theorist on technique. I listened to him and worked really hard on my technique. My club coach at the time, Joe Plant, who was widely recognised in Victoria as a doyen of batting coaches, encouraged me to play attacking shots at practice, to hit through drives and not to block the ball. It was this blend of sound technical instruction and aggressive practice, coupled with watching a model technician, John Shaw, in action that provided the foundation for my success at the first-class level.

MARK TAYLOR claimed he could mimic other players quite easily and was especially impressed with the way Allan Border played. He watched him closely, and the quality he most admired was Border's ability to 'handle the moment, knowing when to attack and when to defend'. **DENE HILLS** spent a lot of time in his early days watching and batting with David Boon. As well as being motivated to earn Boon's respect, Hills believed he modelled himself on many of his techniques and strategies. He said, 'I liked Boony's ability to bat for long periods of time, with quality defence and patience being the keys. I just wanted to bat with him and earn his respect'.

Although **GREG SHIPPERD** adopted his own unique style, he was also influenced by the style and personality of two of his early mentors, Derek Chadwick (ex Western Australian opening bat) and John Inverarity. He said, 'Their stubbornness and toughness at the crease was something that stuck in my mind'.

TIP Batters should watch the best players to form a template for successful batting. Playing straight, blending aggression with a tight technique and enduring tough spells to bat for a lengthy period are some of the lessons they can learn from them.

So, the first step to batting improvement appears to involve watching others closely and trying to adopt some of their techniques or strategies. Although this book is not meant to be a book about techniques, inevitably, the players we interviewed mentioned some aspects of technique that helped them to become better players. As mentioned previously, Ian Redpath was steeped in a sound technique but coupled this with attacking stroke play. Such a view is supported by **JOHN INVERARITY**, whose drills focus on developing a full, uninterrupted swing of the bat (these drills will be outlined in more detail later). Although **BOB SIMPSON** recommended work on technique, he warned about the issue of overcoaching:

> Early on, I assisted with coaching at my club and, through teaching, I learnt something about technique. But still, with children up to 12 years of age, I just taught them grip and stance and let them rely on their own instincts to hit the ball. Overcoaching may not be in the best interests of players.

GREG CHAPPELL believes that the following experience was an essential part of his development and provided him with the best background for the game that he could have:

> Our father always encouraged us to make runs in the backyard. This is where I learned to play a shot off my left hip to hit the ball between the almond and the apricot tree. Having a brother who was five years older than me, and never made any concessions, taught me how to survive and prosper. It certainly helped me when I was under siege against the might of the West Indies during the 1970s and 1980s.

Tight technical instruction must be balanced with encouraging batters to have some flair when hitting the ball. Too much technical emphasis may impede a player's free-flowing stroke play. Too little, of course, may cause the player to fail because of loose technique. Balance is a much sought after commodity in most sports. Dean Jones identified its role in batting by saying, 'If you don't have balance, you don't have power. I liked to adopt a boxer's stance with the bat raised (like the boxer's hands), and feet stable but ready to move'.

Many players we interviewed recognised the need to learn back foot shots. Taylor contrasted the more traditional model of back foot play with the modern approach. He named Matthew Elliott and Steve Waugh as genuine back foot players who used the whole crease to get back close to their stumps to play hooks and cuts. Nowadays, he points to Ricky Ponting (shown in figure 3.1) or Matthew Hayden as using a technique that starts with a decisive forward press and then a rock back to play pull shots in particular. Often, this means that their back foot is on the crease line when they play these shots.

Both Shipperd and Simpson liked to teach players to drive straight down the ground off their back foot as well as to play square of the wicket. Shipperd watched Ponting do this as a youngster, and Simpson admired Norm O'Neill for this stroke. Taylor contended that the bottom hand was a major contributor to cuts and pull shots. Simpson warned that it is very important to play with either a horizontal or straight bat. He believes that many present-day batsmen are playing back foot shots by falling backwards a little with their bat at 45 degrees. The result is that more inside edges are occurring.

On a strategic level, two renowned rotators of the strike, Simpson and Dean Jones, had some advice about the importance of batting partnerships in applying pressure to the bowlers. Simpson claimed that 'the safest place to be is at the other end so that bowlers don't get a chance to get into a plan'. Jones believes that batters need to work with a partner to upset a bowler's length:

Figure 3.1 Ricky Ponting hooking with minimal back foot movement while straddling the crease.

I got a lot of fun out of pinching a single. It needed two class batters to beat a top-class bowler. For example, when playing spin, Boon would play a lot off the back foot, whereas I would run at them. That has to upset their length. Allow a bowler to bowl length and they have got you.

So, armed with these and other technical skills, how have our players gone about developing their game through cutting edge practice? We will now investigate some of the practices adopted by the players interviewed for this book to improve their game.

Batting Practices

Players clearly need to work to refine their skills at training, but they also need to be able to adapt to situations as they occur in matches. This section provides practices used by players to enhance their performance, first at training and then in matches.

Training Practices

This section outlines practices adopted by players in their quest for continued improvement in their batting. We start by investigating practice principles to guide all sessions and then address fundamentals of the grip on the bat and the stance, and how to use net training productively. We then present some specific problems batters face and detail solutions.

Batting Drill Guidelines

To have players practice effectively, coaches need to design drills or activities that optimise skill development. Tom Moody outlined the following excellent guidelines for effective batting drills:

- The drills should be match-specific and have an unpredictable element in them, including variations in the length, line and pace of the ball.
- The drills should be designed to remedy weaknesses as well as practicing strengths.
- Long-term changes in technique require patience and can take up to six months to become effective.
- Players should respect being in form and practice more to reduce the potential for form slumps occurring.
- All players need to feel comfortable playing all strokes including the reverse sweep. (Players may not feel adept enough at all strokes to play in a match situation, but practice should always be geared towards extending their range of strokes.)
- All players should have an understanding of the match plan and their role(s) in executing that plan. Practice then should provide opportunities to play those expected roles.

GRIP ON THE BAT

Interestingly, many players experimented with grip changes at various stages of their careers. Taylor believed that when he was not in form he used to be more aware of his grip. He was always trying to get the bat through as straight as possible, and when that did not happen, he would change his grip slightly. Specifically, players tended to vary the pressure of their grip. Dean Jones claimed that, in tense situations, he really concentrated on grip pressure. He said, 'I tried to hold the bat with a pressure of 2 out of 10—very light. If I had light hands, I had light arms and light shoulders. With that "lightness" I felt I could make a good pass at the ball'. He cited a lesson he learned from his first Test match when he was gripping the bat so tightly that the glue was coming out of the handle!

BELINDA CLARK, like Jones, believed her hands were very sensitive. Sometimes she would pick the bat up and it would feel like a foreign weapon. She tried to monitor the amount of pressure in each hand, with the top hand strong at impact (8 out of 10), and the bottom hand as relaxed as possible for as long as possible. She squeezed the bat with the thumb and forefinger of her bottom hand trying to keep her last three fingers off the bat. Mark Taylor tended to move his hands around the bat, sometimes into a stronger position, sometimes into a weaker position. He also found that his bottom hand used to be a problem if he gripped the bat too strongly:

> Quite often during my career when I was trying to play off drives, I would come through too much with my bottom hand and the ball would hit an inside edge and squirt out to the leg side. I was forever trying to relax the bottom hand without losing power. There were times when I tried gripping the bat with just the thumb and forefinger.

These approaches support the much-publicised technique adopted by Adam Gilchrist when he placed a small soft ball inside his bottom hand, as demonstrated in figure 3.2. By contrast, Shipperd and Hills had unusual grips that they believed still enabled them to play adequately, and so they didn't change them to any extent. Hills said he had a 'funny grip, but I stuck with it because it was comfortable and still allowed me to get the full face of the bat to the ball'. Shipperd, a diminutive player, believed his 'hands apart' grip was effective in countering balls that were reaching him at chest or throat height.

The players we interviewed appear to have experimented with variations of the standard V grip at various stages, and certainly the amount of pressure exerted by the hands was a major factor in their set-up.

STANCE AT THE CREASE

Typically, a side-on stance with the feet placed shoulder-width apart is the most recommended stance. However, on occasions, variations in

Figure 3.2 A small soft ball placed inside the bottom hand of a right-hand batter to release grip pressure. This is a technique that was used successfully by Australian top-order batsman and wicketkeeper, Adam Gilchrist.

this stance may be appropriate. Dean Jones said, 'The quicker the pitch, the closer I'd have my feet together. On a windy day I would spread a bit further to try and hold my balance. Balance is one of the important keys to batting'. Taylor adjusted his stance from the traditional method to a more front-on stance after viewing footage of himself at a local cricket centre. He said, 'I was missing a lot of balls on my pads, so my coach recommended I relax my front shoulder and open my stance a little to help me play on the leg side. That really helped, and I adopted that technique for the rest of my career'. Jones also varied his batting guard from time to time:

> I didn't bat just on leg stump or middle stump. If I was facing Jeff Thomson, I would bat on off stump because I knew that it was impossible for him to get a leg before wicket. Similarly, this approach worked for Wasim Akram when he was bowling around the wicket. For bowlers like Terry Alderman, who got really close to stumps, I would bat on leg stump. You still needed to maintain an awareness of where your off stump was, in order for these variations to work.

MELANIE JONES liked to cock her wrists in the set-up for batting, and made adjustments to the width of her stance as she became more experienced. Her initial narrow stance was modelled from Sharon Tredrea, who was an Australian champion at the time. Melanie eventually became comfortable with the more traditional shoulder-width stance.

NET PRACTICE

Because replicating match conditions in the traditional net situation is difficult, players have to be innovative in their preparation. Clark did a lot of throw-downs in the nets and had a good technical coach from the age of 14. She performed a lot of tasks that involved hitting the ball to precise spots. Melanie Jones focused on power and placement drills by changing the pace of shots to create a wider range of scoring options. She used posts in the nets or cones as targets to indicate either gaps or fielders, as shown in figure 3.3. **TOM MOODY** extended this concept during centre wicket practice when he placed cones in the outfield and had the players hit the ball with control to these zones to practice controlled boundary hitting.

Taylor believed that he often lost control of his shots by trying to hit the ball too hard. So, in the nets he concentrated on keeping his front elbow up and pushed the ball through the covers for two or three runs rather than trying to smash it to the boundary. In this way, he kept the bat straight, presenting the ball with its full face. Belinda Clark concurred with Taylor and warned that players tended to overplay in the nets, particularly when batting to a bowling machine. She said, 'In the nets, I'd really concentrate on not trying to overhit. Correct execution and feel of the ball on the bat was more important than having the ball flying out of the net everywhere. Touch and the ability to change the speed of the ball were my focus'. Incidentally, Clark also attributes her undoubted ability

Figure 3.3 Net training with cones in position to simulate the position of fielders. Cones of one colour (yellow) indicate close fielders, and those of another colour (orange) indicate fielders deeper than 30 metres from the batter.

to work the ball, with adroit use of her wrists, to her background in tennis and hockey (see figure 3.4 for an example of using a hockey stick to refine eye–hand coordination in cricket):

> I played a lot of tennis till I was about 16 years of age. With hours of practice and exploration of new skills, I developed a lot of touch which I think transferred to my batting. Also, I did a lot of bouncing the ball off a hockey stick, and I think that helped in development of my eye–hand coordination in cricket.

Figure 3.4 Using a hockey stick to refine eye–hand coordination.

The challenge of playing quality bowling in the nets can be daunting for some, particularly on poor wickets. However, Ian Redpath believed that he was fortunate to have Test players Alan Connolly, Ian Meckiff and Ian Quick bowling to him at club practice for South Melbourne. His confidence in playing at a higher level grew as he first learned to survive against them and then ultimately attack their bowling. Redpath also used the nets to practice dropping the ball for short singles by taking the bottom hand off the bat. Good length balls in particular were dropped on the leg side, and in his mind he would think, 'There's a run there'.

Batters are often tempted to make the most of every minute of their time in the nets by playing a shot at every ball. Several players alluded to the importance of letting the ball go through to the keeper in net situations. Clark did drills in which she would have to leave the ball and call out whether it was going to hit the stumps. Taylor used to segment his practice time in the following way:

> I used to think of the first five minutes of net practice as the first 30 minutes of my innings. I would leave the ball a lot and wouldn't play a big drive or cut until I had played about 20 to 30 balls in the nets. Eventually, when I started to pick up the ball a bit better and my feet were moving well, I would start playing in a more aggressive manner.

TIP Players should approach the first few minutes of net practice in the same way as the first stages of an innings. They should start cautiously and then gradually become more aggressive as they see the ball better and move more fluently.

PRACTICING UNINHIBITED SWINGS OF THE BAT

John Inverarity questioned the traditional method of teaching a sound defence before developing attacking shots. He developed specific drills that are clearly better suited to the demands of the modern game. Because Inverarity has believed for some time that a defensive shot is merely the stopping of an attacking shot, he advocates drills that provide the opportunity for players to hit with a full, uninhibited swing, as shown in figure 3.5 (A description of these drills is on a Coaching Guide CD available through Cricket Australia.) Batters in limited over matches are now measured on their strike rates, and so the ability to hit the ball is perhaps more important than a tight defence. Among the modern players, perhaps Andrew Symonds illustrates this approach more than any other. His game is built on his ability to hit the ball powerfully. It was only in the latter half of his career that he has learned the balance needed between offence and defence to succeed at Test level.

The drills are aimed at overcoming any tendency to rotate and open up the hips too early, which can result in hitting across the line of the ball. This can also inhibit the freedom of the bat swing and the ability to strike the ball cleanly. The drills encourage the batter to execute a full and natural

Figure 3.5 Final progression in Inverarity drills in which the thrower makes an underarm throw to a batter, who practices a full uninhibited bat swing.

bat swing while maintaining a consistent body position until just before striking the ball. They are relevant for beginners as well as experienced players who are having difficulty with their technique.

The drills commence with the batter striking a ball that has been rolled along the pitch over a distance of 8 to 10 metres, and they progress to striking a ball that has either been thrown or released from a bowling machine to bounce on the pitch before reaching the batter. Although practicing the drills is different from batting in a match, the skills acquired may translate readily to match situations. They are aimed at helping a batter learn an optimum feel in terms of body movements and positions and bat swing. Effective learning can take place from recognising and repeating the 'good feel' elements of striking the ball. The drills are not difficult to perfect, but they require a partner with good throwing skills to roll or throw the ball accurately and at the right pace.

USING BALL DROPS

This approach, in which the coach drops the ball into a hitting position for the batter, has been used more extensively by female cricketers in Australia as an alternative to the traditional way of preparing for batting (see figure 3.6). Perhaps this drill is based at a more fundamental level, but like the previous Inverarity batting drills, it is aimed at promoting bat swing from

Figure 3.6 Coach John Buchanan doing ball drops for the sweep shot of Adam Gilchrist.

a stable base. Ball drops can be used to practice both front and back foot shots. The idea is to groove a balanced swing while checking that the hands are working effectively to present the full face of the bat to the ball. Clark started using ball drops when she was 18 years old, and she believed it was an effective way of training because it didn't require a lot of resources or effort in feeding. She stressed that this was just an adjunct to other methods that she used.

One of the major limitations of this drill is that the ball is not delivered towards the batter but is dropped vertically. Therefore, batters do not practice tracking a ball coming towards them as they have to do in a match.

USING THROW-DOWNS AND BOWLING MACHINES

It is more difficult than ever to replicate the bowling motion in batting sessions, because bowlers' workloads are constantly monitored to prevent overuse injuries. As a result, players resort to having throw-downs or the ball delivered from a bowling machine. With throw-downs, players may protect their arms and propel the ball at a much slower pace than that experienced in a match. CATHRYN FITZPATRICK alluded to this problem when she said, 'I hated underarm throws and always wanted the ball pinged at me'.

The bowling machine clearly has its value because it can provide a lot of blocked or random practice. Blocked practice essentially enables the batter to repeat a stroke over and over to consolidate a particular skill. In random practice, the ball machine's length, line, pace or movement may vary with each delivery to closely replicate a match situation. However, it is obvious to batters that changes are being made, which does not allow them to focus on important bowling cues at ball release. Also, the use of plastic cricket balls without seams limits the value of bowling machines for specifically preparing batters for competition.

USING BATTING AIDS

Clark practiced a lot as a youngster with a skinny bat more by chance than design. That was the bat that the kids on the street used. She believed it helped shape her good technique and ensured that she watched the ball closely. This strategy has been used more frequently at the elite level in recent times. The idea is to narrow the hitting area to ensure that when batters play strokes with a larger bat, they make contact closer to the sweet spot.

Practices to Solve Specific Problems

From time to time, players confront situations in matches that indicate the need to adapt their approach to be more successful. This section addresses some of these issues and suggests approaches players can adopt to ensure their practices are productive. In addition, ways of developing a grooved, full-bat swing, without the use of bowlers, are outlined.

COMBATING A REVERSE SWING

A reverse swing in cricket bowling has been a recent phenomenon that has challenged batters. Dean Jones recommends that batters practice in the following way: 'Watch the ball a little bit more, don't move your feet, and with your feet together, just hit through the line of the ball. The bowlers are trying to get you out either bowled or leg before wicket, and if you move your front foot towards mid off, then you are setting yourself up for one of those methods of dismissal'.

DEALING WITH A LOSS OF FORM

Setting out to play with controlled aggression was a key remedy for many batters when dealing with a loss of form. Simpson preferred the term *mental aggression* to *physical aggression*. The latter, he claims, results in players wanting to belt the ball, but what he advocated was to be mentally after the ball with controlled aggression, whether you hit it for one, two or four runs. A sense of conviction in one's strokes is important here, and particularly when players become tentative during form lapses.

Redpath would try to play more aggressively in the nets, working on getting into good position and swinging the bat properly. He believed that he sometimes became a little lazy in his concentration on those basics, and usually just switching them on was enough to turn things around.

DECIDING WHEN TO CUT

Shipperd used this strategy in deciding whether he could safely cut a ball: 'In my mind I would have a length and width of a ball that was suitable to cut. If the ball was fuller than that or inside the width line, I would play with a straighter bat either defensively or in an attacking manner. So it was about having the channels of line and length that gave me a cue that a cut shot was on'.

Although for the most part cricketers need to practice diligently for many hours to hone their skills, physical and mental burnout can occur in some cases when athletes overtrain. Taylor warned that sometimes players need to 'do less rather than more'. He cited a time when he was in poor form with the bat in his third season in State cricket. One of his mentors, Neil Marks, made the following suggestion to reduce his workload and freshen him up. Marks stated, 'I think you are running around the block more than you ever used to, and I bet you are getting more time in the nets than you were last year. And you can't make a run, can you? Well, I've got some advice. Pack your bat, pads and gloves in your cricket bag and stick it under your bed for two weeks. Come back when you're ready to enjoy the game'.

 Coaches must ensure that players are fresh for matches. Using ball machines and throw-downs can lighten the load on bowlers and provide some variations in batting practice, which can assist this process during the lead-up period.

Training in the Week Prior to a Match

The training focus changes at various times throughout a season of cricket. For example, preseason training is different from the training that is geared towards an upcoming match. Club players typically have a week of preparation for specific opposition, whereas International players with busier schedules may have less time between matches. Whatever the level of cricket, players must be prepared for the specific style of game and for a specific opposition. They should have a sense of gearing up for a match both physically and mentally.

Players have different things they like to do in the week prior to a match. Some like to work harder on skills, whereas others prefer to lighten their load to freshen up for the contest. Belinda Clark addressed the need to strike a balance between 'psyching up' and 'psyching down' for an upcoming contest. She said, 'I needed to have a couple of long hits to make sure I had done the physical work. Outside of that, I didn't want to get too intense about the contest. I did my preparation early in the week, and in the day or two before the game, I wanted to relax'.

Ian Healy wanted to be clear headed and focused on watching the ball and responding. He worked on seeing the ball and moving to the length and wanted to be in an aggressive frame of mind. Bob Simpson tried to get into the mindset of playing in a match. He competed against the bowlers in the nets and didn't want to get out or play a bad shot. He batted with fielders in position in his own mind and would say, 'That's a two' or 'That's hit straight to the fielder'. The volume of practice accomplished in the week prior to the match was important to Greg Shipperd. He just loved to prepare and enjoyed the company of the squad. He would practice hitting balls as much as he could. The need to replicate the specifics of his role and the conditions he would expect to confront were foremost in Mark Taylor's preparation:

> I used to like having quality net sessions and would request the fastest bowlers because I was an opening batter. It was particularly desirable to practice on wickets that were similar to what you would get in the game. Perth and India were two examples where practice on their unique style of wicket was critical in the week before a big game. In Perth, you can sometimes let a ball go that pitches on the stumps because traditionally there is extra bounce in that wicket. By practicing on similar conditions, you were conditioning your mind to play that way in the game.

By contrast, sometimes the practice wickets are so poor that confidence can be eroded, as Dene Hills found with Hobart wickets in his time. He therefore kept his preparation simple and made sure that he did not lose confidence, often relying on mental practice to prepare him for competition. Hills said, 'I mentally visualised the bowlers coming at me. In the nets I had a few throw-downs and faced a few bowlers but mainly focused on moving well to the ball. It was a relief to get out in the middle because the wicket was true, and with decent sight screens, your vision was much better'.

It appears that players need to take practice conditions into account before making any commitment to a practice routine prior to a match. If practice pitches are substantially different from what a batter may expect in the match, then there may be more benefit derived from practicing on an artificial surface. Players want to feel confident going into a match, and underprepared pitches may make it difficult to feel good about their game.

Match Practices

Once the match starts, players need to be adaptable to the uncertainty of the match. However, most will develop routines that make them feel more comfortable and prepared. This section outlines some of these routines.

PRE-INNINGS

Once a player gets to the ground, there is an opportunity to engage both the mind and the body in getting ready to bat. As expected, the players we interviewed developed their own routines while being mindful of team needs as well. In the one to one-and-a-half hours of active time typically used to prepare for a day of cricket, players need to be mindful of the multitude of roles they may play and prepare both body and mind as well as they can. The following section offers some insights on the warm-up preferences of players interviewed for this book.

Warm-Up

Clark, who captained a team for most of her career, had to combine the roles of captain and opening batter in the prematch period. She decided to break her routine into two phases—before the toss she focused on physical preparation, and after the toss she focused on mental preparation. The physical preparation phase generally went as follows:

> I liked to run and stretch and be physically warm before skill work. Then I would like to catch before I hit, maybe 10 short catches with my pads on but without gloves. Then I would hit a few, and my focus was more on engaging my feet than on striving for perfect contact. I wanted to feel my hands relaxed with a clear mind.

Several other players liked to do some catching before batting. Hills made sure he had a few sharp catches to sharpen his reflexes and to track the ball. Although most of the players we interviewed had access to nets, many didn't feel the need for extensive skill practice just before the match. Redpath just wanted to hit the ball cleanly to give him some confidence. If he didn't hit it well, it didn't worry him that much, but he was probably a bit more circumspect when he went out to bat. Ironically, he claimed that a lot of his best innings were linked to warm-ups in which he hadn't hit the ball all that well. He just fought harder to concentrate in these times and reaped the rewards.

Taylor and Simpson tended to have net practice on the morning prior to a Test match. However, Taylor said that if he was in good form, often a few throw-downs would suffice. His focus was more on getting his mind right for the contest and simply trying to get his feet moving in the physical part of his warm-up. Chappell's priority was also to make sure that he was thinking positively, which he could control, and he spent more time ensuring that this was the case than he did on the physical side of the warm-up. He said, 'I only had a quick hit or took a couple of good catches on the day of the match and then stopped. You can train yourself out of form just as easily as you can train yourself into form'.

Because most average club players do not have access to nets prior to a match, it is important to understand the key focal areas in this situation. Hills believes we have a lot to explore in this area. As a player, he did what everyone else did— practiced against bowlers in a net or used throw-downs either on the field or on a pitch just to get the body moving. However, at the Cricket Australia Centre of Excellence, he has tried many ways to get players ready to compete. He has used skipping ropes to enhance foot movement, had players hit a ball on a string for enhanced ball focus and tried the Bradman technique of hitting a ball with a cricket stump. Many of these innovations in match preparation are difficult to introduce to senior players who have become settled into their prematch routines. Experience would suggest that these players should go through their normal routines, but that the search for improved ways of preparation should be ongoing and probably directed at younger players.

Shipperd's approach to prematch preparation was a continuation of his normal practice routine. He was a strong believer in the throw-down and ball machine processes and liked to have 10 minutes on the machine practicing around the entire circumference of scoring possibilities. Then he would follow with 15 minutes of throw-downs and 10 minutes facing bowlers.

The warm-up for batting is governed by time and resource limitations, tradition and player preferences. There may be much to learn in this area from other sports such as tennis and golf. Tennis players typically have a thorough skill warm-up for up to two hours or more before competition. Golfers also hit a lot of balls on the practice range before each round. As more innovative approaches are introduced, players may decide that they need to do more than hit a few balls to get ready to perform. Cricket, however, is such a difficult game for which to prepare because, unlike golf, there is seldom a precise 'tee time'.

This brings us to the exploration of how players use their time once they have their pads on and are waiting either for the umpires to let them know that the innings is about to begin, or for a wicket to fall.

Waiting to Bat

Nervous, expectant, fearful, hopeful, determined, agitated, listless, worried and confident are just a few of the ways batters may feel while waiting their turn to bat. For this reason, what players do and think prior to their innings to cope with these responses is vitally important. Because the challenge of being ready to compete but not 'over the top' remains a constant issue for batters at all levels of cricket, it is fascinating to examine what the greats of the game have done in this period.

Many of the players we interviewed reported a sense of trusting their preparation as they got their minds and bodies ready for the battle ahead. Some did so by relaxing as much as possible, whereas others were more likely to get their adrenaline pumping. Clearly, players' approaches to getting ready to bat depended on previous successes; for example, if a batter had made runs after a certain process was in place, he would be more likely to maintain that approach in future. Many players use a simplistic mindset. Cathryn Fitzpatrick's role was typically to get things moving in the middle order. Her dictum was to 'see it and hit it', and she would have that thought in her mind prior to batting. Having a clear head is a desirable state, as Simpson explained:

> I like to be relaxed, as I had done all my thinking the night before on how to handle different types of bowlers and so on. I tried to pull out the computer information from the night before when it became appropriate. On the day of the game, I liked to have a clear mind, have quick reactions and trust the computer (mind).

By contrast, if Redpath was opening the batting, he was jumping out of his skin, intent on surviving rather than playing too aggressively:

> The adrenaline was important at that time of my innings. I would try to get the right thoughts in my mind—thinking of surviving the first 30 minutes by leaving the ball alone, lowering my potential for mistakes. I used to be more instinctive and play more aggressively as a youngster, but I found I had to adjust as bowlers started to direct the ball to where I didn't want it.

Figure 3.7 Melanie Jones, demonstrating a decisive square cut, was prepared to play her core shots early in her innings.

Melanie Jones, as shown in figure 3.7, spoke of having a match plan set in her mind during the week to combat particular bowlers, much like Simpson. She focused on core shots rather than braver shots at the start of her innings. She would be prepared to drive, cut and pull early because she trusted those shots at any time. Also, she was very conscious as she waited to go in to bat of setting her mind for drop and run shots to rotate the strike.

Other opening batters tended to come prepared for batting first but recognised that the toss of the coin either sharpened their focus or delayed it for a period. Hills alluded to the problem that the traditional late toss of the coin causes opening batters. Not knowing whether you are batting or bowling is far from ideal.

Both Clark and Taylor had to deal with opening the batting and captaining a side. Clark's approach also emphasised the need for a clear mind. She ensured that her thoughts were clear and narrow by focusing on watching the ball. She wanted to be in a space in which she wasn't too nervous or concerned and reinforced the positives. She did not worry about conditions, opposition bowlers or the score but just went back to the basics. She would tell herself, 'I am going to watch the ball and have fun'. However, Taylor and Clark both alluded to the problem of opening the batting on a changeover of innings, after they had been in the field for some time. Clark found this very challenging, particularly when she was actively engaged in the field as captain. She preferred to get ready very quickly and practice hitting some balls, still going through her process, albeit an abbreviated one. She needed the physical practice to get her mind in the right place.

Batting down the order also produces unique problems for batters, not the least of which is the uncertainty of when they will be asked to bat. Greg Shipperd, who batted a lot at number three in the order, used to focus on specific conditions:

> I looked at the bounce of the ball as it passed the batter and the carry through to the wicketkeeper. Also, I noted the wind direction and considered how I could use the wind to my advantage. I would look for the amount of swing, seam or spin that the bowlers were getting and adjust my plan as a result. Often, I would go out at lunchtime if we were batting and waiting to bat, and I would look at where the bowlers had been landing the ball mostly.

The amount of social contact players want during the waiting time varies. Some like to be engaged with others because it relaxes them. Others, like Dean Jones, prefer to be involved in positive thoughts and observing what the bowlers are doing. He was very easily annoyed by negative talk by fellow players:

> I don't want blokes saying that X is bowling fast or that the pitch is doing a lot. If they are saying that, I would tell them to shut up or I would move away. Such negativity impacts on your thinking. Also, I am trying to watch how the ball is being released from the bowler's hands, and in particular I'm really trying to watch the length that is being bowled. You can have the perfect technique,

but if you can't read the length of the ball as it is released and if you go forward to a ball that is short, you are in trouble.

This view is shared by Greg Chappell, who believed that worrying about the opposition bowlers and the pitch conditions was a waste of emotional energy and could destroy an innings before it commenced. He used a car analogy to identify three levels of concentration required while batting: idling before commencing to bat and between deliveries, first gear after a wicket falls or when the bowler starts the approach to the wicket and full throttle as the ball is released from the bowler's hand.

Justin Langer, as shown in figure 3.8, has distinct routines that he follows to get into what he terms the 'ready zone' when he is preparing to bat. He stated, 'I place my helmet, chewing gum and water bottle in the same position alongside me and listen to music on my iPod. This helps me relax'.

 Coaches need to be aware of the characteristics of individual players when evaluating their immediate pre-match routines. Each person is unique. Equally, players need to be educated about appropriate methods of getting ready for competition.

Figure 3.8 Justin Langer with headphones on, waiting to go in to bat, in company with teammate and pace bowler Glenn McGrath.

STARTING AN INNINGS

Establishing an innings with a solid foundation is critical to batting success. Shipperd indicated that his approach was one of caution that perhaps would not be accepted in the modern game:

> I approached the start of my innings with caution, with my priority to maintain my wicket and build a foundation. I think that has changed for the better these days, but in my time and with my skill set and the demands of the team, I chose to play more conservatively. I played at a time when fast bowling around the world was more consistent and stronger, so there was a place for someone to adopt an anchor role. Nowadays, players such as Michael Hussey, who can anchor an innings if required, also have the ability to lift a gear and play at different paces.

Redpath and Taylor also predominantly tended to follow this conservative approach to the start of their innings. Redpath attributed this approach not only to the state of mind of the batter, but also to the quality of modern bats. In his day, a slight mistiming of a stroke would court danger, but these strokes today seem to land over the infield. Taylor wanted bowlers to bowl to his strengths, so early on he let a lot of balls go through to the keeper:

> I used to like the bowlers to bowl the ball to me, rather than looking to play a cover drive or a square cut in the first 10 to 20 runs. I would hope the bowlers would then bowl more at the stumps in the hope that I could work them through the leg side in a safer manner. I waited until I got to the stage where I felt my eye was in and my feet were moving well before I played more expansively.

Right at the start of her innings, Clark was conscious of following her routine, marking and checking centre before a little walk to the side. She focused on relaxing her body sufficiently and being in a positive frame of mind so that if there was a ball to be hit, she did so. However, she tried very hard not to pre-empt any shots. She said, 'I found if I tried to pre-empt shots, I would miss other opportunities to score. If I had six good balls delivered and I had to play them safely for no runs, then I was confident I could catch that up later. So I tried to play each ball on its merits'.

Simpson also advocated a reactionary, rather than pre-emptive approach. Also, in contrast to others mentioned earlier, if he was served up a long hop first ball, he would try to cut it (although he did admit that he would not go as hard at the ball early in his innings) and use the pace of the ball to score with that stroke. Melanie Jones, however, liked to feel the bat on the ball and tried to impose herself on the opposition by being decisive in all her movements and use her voice with conviction in all her calls to her batting partner. The early stages of an innings are clearly the most challenging ones, and as Chappell pointed out, 60 percent of batters don't make 20 runs. He said, 'Don Bradman was no better than anyone else for the first 20 minutes, and Brian Lara knew that he could make a big score if he could last 60 balls'.

Developing Partnerships

Building partnerships is considered essential in producing big scores. Clearly, partnerships can consist of players who are just good individual players. However, if the two players actually enjoy each other's company and have game styles that complement each other, then the partnership is potentially even more powerful.

As shown in figure 3.9, Justin Langer shared an opening partnership with Matthew Hayden that was the most successful in Australian Test cricket history and included six double century stands. In the following quote Langer outlines the factors, other than talent, that contributed to their success:

> Our partnership was based on true friendship and respect. It was real Aussie mateship, and we were always ready to pat each other on the back or tell each other off. We bonded well because we have similar interests and a similar philosophy based on a strong work ethic. We had similar career paths in that, at some stage, both of us had lost our places in the Test side and had to fight hard to improve our games, regain our places and stay there. . . . Even though we were both left-handers, we had contrasting batting styles. Matthew was more of a front-of-the-wicket player, whereas I tended to play more square of the wicket shots. This made it difficult for the bowlers, who had to continually adjust their line and length when we were batting together.

Figure 3.9 Justin Langer and Matthew Hayden celebrating one of their many memorable opening partnerships for Australia.

MAKING PRELIMINARY MOVEMENTS

Traditional cricket wisdom has it that a batter needs to wait until the ball's length is known before the feet move either back or forward to play an appropriate shot. However, observation of most elite players indicates that a preliminary movement occurs at or before ball release. Whether this movement is back or forward appears to be a matter of individual preference throughout our recent history.

Dean Jones reported a conversation with Sir Donald Bradman about preliminary movements in which Bradman said that a car needs a starter motor to get the big engines moving. In this sense the preliminary movement is akin to a waggle before a golf swing; it seems to set the swing in motion. Jones himself had a unique movement pattern with his right foot going across to the off side and forward almost towards cover and his front foot going in the direction of the bowler. When he batted poorly, he claimed his back foot went up and down on the one spot and his front foot went to mid off.

Chappell's view is that batters must expect the ball to be full length, in which case the body is readied for forward movement by unweighting the front foot slightly. This should not be seen as a commitment to a front foot plant as the ball is released, but merely prepares the body for movement. Should the ball be pitched short, Chappell believes that batters naturally adjust by pushing back onto the back foot.

Two modern trends in batting don't impress Chappell. In the preset stance that many players adopt, the weight is slightly forward and the bat is raised. Unless the ball is bowled in one particular spot, the batter will be in the wrong place. Chappell has studied footage of many elite players and contends that they set the body position as late as possible. He also does not support the approach that has the front foot moving with a small stride straight down the wicket. He believes this sets batters up to play with the hands away from the body with a gap between bat and pad, which makes them vulnerable to the ball moving away from them. With front foot shots, the batter must try to keep the ball on the off side of the front leg. This keeps the batter in a perfect state of balance because the head will be taken to the line of the ball. Also, the bat will have a clear path to the ball without having to go around the front pad.

A number of players adopted a back foot initial movement. Redpath moved back and across initially in an innings and believed he may have adjusted that as his innings progressed. When the bowling was quick, he would try to get farther back. Clark had continuing issues with her preliminary movements:

> Innately, I moved my back foot back and across. If I wasn't playing well, often I found I went too far across and exposed my leg stump. Later on I tried to go forward more to stop going too far across. I often asked the other batter for feedback on my preliminary movements. To spinners, I unweighted my front foot because my intention against spinners was to get down the pitch to them as much as possible.

Shipperd adopted a back foot initial movement but doesn't coach that now. He went back as far as he could to give himself more time to see the bounce of the ball. Brought up on the bouncy WACA pitch, Shipperd was wise enough to adapt to other pitches he confronted in Australia by moving forward first. Conversely, Simpson and Taylor preferred a little step forward to initiate their movements. Simpson favoured a small forward press but emphasised that this was not a commitment that locked him to staying on the front foot. Taylor made some interesting observations about his inability to get deep enough in the crease:

> I'd always have a little step forward with my front foot and then just rock back from there. I would have loved to have a bigger step back and always admired Michael Slater and Matthew Elliott, who had the ability to get well back. I tried to do this with a big step back first, but I found it threw my balance out and I couldn't get my feet anywhere near enough to good position. So, after three weeks of trying, I reverted to my previous approach.

Among the group of players interviewed for this book, there seems to be no clear pattern of preliminary movements. All players, however, did indicate that they had a preliminary movement. This pattern seems to exist with contemporary players, although most seem to adopt a forward press initially. It is clear that elite players are constantly thinking of ways to improve their games, and so they embark on drill sessions to achieve a higher level of performance.

Although tinkering with techniques is often necessary when flaws are apparent in competition, **IAN HEALY** delivered a sage warning about the most appropriate time to make changes to techniques. He didn't like changing much during the competitive season but did try to focus on technical aspects in the off-season. Periodically, he would lose confidence and striking power through the covers and hence worked principally on keeping a high elbow and using his top hand more productively. Usually, this would take a week of intense practice to rectify.

Mental Skills in Batting

Players often have a thought preceding an action. Such thoughts should be positive and related to the intended performance. This section is an adjunct to material presented in chapter 2, Mental Preparation.

Focusing on the Task

The ability to concentrate for long periods is a prerequisite for success in batting. Players adopt a variety of strategies to narrow their attention to the essentials of the task. Clark indicated that, although she needed to be aware of the scoreboard, her primary focus was on keeping herself in the moment. The match was essentially a contest between bat and ball at that moment. She worked hard on shutting down other things competing for her thoughts such as talk from the opposition or the threat of rain.

Justin Langer also was resolute in devoting all of his attention to the next ball:

> I trusted my routine and wanted to respond in the same way to the first ball as I did to the 300th ball. Mental toughness is about giving 100 per cent attention to the next ball bowled. One can never afford to take liberties with concentration. The only thing that matters to me is seeing the ball out of the bowler's fingers, not the expression on his face or how fast he is running.

Simpson also learned that the secret was to reduce peak concentration to a minimum time, and that was when the bowler was in the delivery stride. At that point he said to himself, 'NOW' and then watched the ball come out of the bowler's hand. If players did that for a whole day of play, they would be concentrated fully for only about half an hour.

Although the concept of narrowing attention is common to most elite batters, some strategies do not work for all players, as Ian Healy found when he tried to copy Chappell's method. Chappell used to set short-term goals of making 10 runs at a time. When Healy tried this approach, when he achieved a subgoal of 20 runs, 30 runs seemed a long way off and he would often try to hit his way to that new target. So 'One ball at a time' became Healy's mantra.

Building on Chappell's process of setting short-term targets, Hills liked to focus on the partnership he was developing with Jamie Cox. He would say, 'Good, we've got to 50; now let's keep it going and not get carried away'.

Another method is not to concentrate on anything and just quiet the mind. Redpath used to find himself whistling under his breath so that he was relaxed and trusting of his instincts. Later in his career, as he built up a history with opposition teams, he used to grind his teeth and work very hard to dislike the opposition bowlers.

Batters find different ways to concentrate on the task in hand. Ultimately, the process entails narrowing one's focus to the essentials of the task, while eliminating inappropriate cues.

Creating a Positive Mindset

Although it is important to focus on the task, a player's intent can still vary from day to day. For instance, a player may come out to bat with good focus, but if she has a passive, defensive mindset, she still may not be able to score quickly enough.

Dean Jones had a very positive, attacking mindset when he went out to bat. He was intent on upsetting the length of bowlers and wanted to get the captain of the opposition to move fielders from positions that threatened him. For example, if bat-pad fielders were in place, he would go out with the intent of advancing down the pitch and hitting the ball over the infield to force the captain to adopt a more defensive field. This often created more opportunity for singles and also reduced the threat of bat-pad fielders.

The pressure of maintaining a spot in a team often prevents players from executing their aggressive intents. Shipperd claimed that only later in his career, when he felt his place in the team was secure, was he able to bring himself to use his feet to spinners. This pattern is so often seen when players are new additions to teams. The fear of failure tends to override the aggressive intent of these players, and as a result they often exhibit tentative behaviours.

Dealing With Success and Failure

Simpson adopted a positive view of both success and failure. If he failed three times in a row, he would say to himself, 'I don't normally have three failures in a row, so I am due for a score'. On the other hand, if he made a century, he would say, 'Great, I'm in good form; let's get another'. Redpath believed that when he got out to 'dumb shots', he usually responded by 'getting a bit nasty and more determined'.

Most players experience a slump in form at one time or another. In recent times, approaching the twilight of their careers, two Australian captains, Chappell and Taylor, experienced well-publicised slumps that no doubt challenged their mental strength. Taylor talked frankly about the torment he endured and the innings that turned things around for him:

> Looking back to 1997, I tried a lot of things. I had people writing to me offering me free eye tests and free reaction tests and all sorts of stuff. During that time when you are having a really bad spell, lots of things go through your mind. You get yourself in a situation that you feel as though no matter what you do, things are going to go against you. You're going to find a way of getting out.

> I got to a stage where I couldn't buy a run, no matter what I tried. I tried hitting my way out of it, I tried occupying the crease out of it, almost giving away pull shots just to stay in and hope that something would happen. Eventually, I remember walking out to bat at Edgbaston, that first Test in 1997, and in the second innings, I thought that I was going to make a conscious effort to look around and just enjoy it, really take my mind off it and just see what comes, I suppose.

> Fortunately for me, because they led by something like 370 on the first innings of that game, England came out and tried to bowl us out. And that really played into my hands. I made my first 50 in that innings off 56 balls, 47 of which were scored through the on side. They had forgotten to bowl just full and outside off stump.

> This situation taught me that you have to go back to plan A, and that was probably thrust back on to me by England, because of the way they bowled. My plan was always to leave the ball outside off stump, get bowlers to bowl at the stumps and work leg side until I was playing well enough to play drives. That was my basic game plan, and that was the way I played in that innings.

In performance declines, the mind can even destroy the best of us. Taylor's famous slump demonstrates how a player is always only one innings away from turning things around. Whether it be by good fortune or just sheer persistence, self-confidence can return quickly. In Taylor's case, he had tried other strategies that may have been successful for others, but they didn't work for him. He simply went back to playing the way he knew best.

> **TIP** Being able to deal with failure requires resiliency and self-belief, two characteristics associated with mental toughness. Players who desire long-term success in the game must acquire this attribute.

Summary

On a good day, a batter can spend a lengthy period of time at the crease during a match. To prepare for this, the practice workload must be much greater than that experienced in a short net session. This chapter explores some options to enhance the technical and mental skills involved in match-day batting. These include using ball machines, throw-downs and ball drops as well as employing specific strategies to prepare the mind and body for competition.

Some of the specific recommendations for conducting batting practices are as follows:

- Develop a comprehensive range of both individual and match-related skills and remedy individual limitations, while taking account of the batter's expected role in the team.
- Encourage experimentation with different grip pressures on the bat. Batters should adjust their stance and batting guards to allow for different conditions of the pitch or bowling lines.
- Challenge batters to practice in ways that replicate match situations. They can practice ball placement and power with targets indicating where fielders are positioned. They should resist the temptation to overhit shots in the nets and should value keeping their wicket intact.
- Divide the practice time in the nets into segments of a typical innings. Such segments would include the start of the innings, the period from 20 to 40 runs and the time when the batter is well established with the field in defensive positions. Practice for various versions of the game also requires specific preparation.
- Encourage batters who are down on form to play with conviction and controlled aggression to make sure they do not become too tentative.
- Use bat swing exercises for players to learn the feel and balance required for smooth stroke play.
- Use throw-downs and ball machine work to give batters the volume of work required to groove all strokes.
- Encourage batters to develop routines that prepare them for competition. Having quality specific training, maintaining a clear head, engaging in mental practice and being confident in their batting skills are some of the key factors identified by elite players.

Some of the practices recommended for competition matches are as follows:

- Allow for individual pre-innings preferences, which include some physical skill practice, clearing of the mind and some foot movement drills. As well as preparing themselves physically, players need to get their minds focused on the task ahead. Although some players just want to get a feel for batting, others require a more thorough prematch preparation.

- Encourage batters to establish a preshot routine before each delivery and to adopt a secure way to start an innings.

- Have batters practice a preliminary movement that acts as a trigger for each stroke.

- Encourage batters to develop the mental skills required to enhance concentration, have an aggressive intent, commit to a batting routine and deal with both failure and success.

- Every batter is unique in terms of level of technical skill, mental and physical capabilities and commitment to individual and team training and performance. What works for some may not work for others. Coaches need to recognise this when preparing a team for competition.

CHAPTER 4

Bowling

Throughout history many bowling actions have been used to achieve success at all levels of cricket. On the international front we have witnessed and respected great diversity within a single team. Recall the Australian attack of the 1970s of Dennis Lillee (pure side-on action), Jeff Thomson (slinging super side-on action) and Max Walker (front-on action). Contrast that to more recent times when Glen McGrath, Shane Warne, Brett Lee and Jason Gillespie headed the Australian attack. From swing bowlers to seamers, wrist spinners to finger spinners, coaches have traditionally guided youngsters in their formative bowling years to bowl with a side-on action.

In recent times the proclivity to injury in many of our bowlers has resulted in a thorough analysis of bowling actions, with safer techniques now the norm. Mixed actions, in which the top half of the body is not aligned with the bottom half, have been changed to either side-on or front-on actions. Workloads of pace bowlers, in particular, have been closely monitored to help prevent overuse injuries. As a result of all this scrutiny, players have had to work harder on making modifications to their bowling action at practice. Drills have been developed to assist this process, and many of these are presented in this chapter.

In addition to becoming safer, bowling has also evolved in terms of the variety of deliveries. Doosras have become almost mandatory for orthodox spinners since the rules on actions (now allowing some elbow bend) have been relaxed. Reverse swing has become a key focus for pace bowlers once the ball has lost its new shine. 'Flippers' and 'zooters' have become part of wrist spinners' armouries as they continue to explore ways to confuse batters with their subtle variations. These changes have meant that bowlers have had to keep working on extending their skill range while striving for control. Such an approach demands specific practice.

This chapter examines the processes bowlers have adopted to bowl in a manner that is safe and consistent, yet threatening. It is not sufficient just to bowl a lot of balls at training. The ability to monitor their action and modify it if control or venom are lacking is of paramount concern to modern bowlers.

Bowling Skills and Strategies

Bowlers must understand the principles governing a sound bowling action. A mechanically sound technique can do much to ensure long-term involvement in the game with minimal interruption as a result of injury. As well, efficiency of technique can produce more effective outcomes in terms of generating power, spin or swing. Although it was not a major focus of this book to provide a comprehensive analysis of the skill of bowling, the players we interviewed mentioned some key aspects of technique, which we have summarised.

Pace Bowling

Quality pace bowling requires a smooth and accelerating run-up, a powerful and efficient bowling action and the capability to vary the line, length and speed of deliveries according to the perceived weaknesses of the batters and the circumstances of the game.

RUN-UP

Because research has shown that the run-up in pace bowlers contributes approximately 20 per cent to the velocity of the ball, there has been more emphasis on bowlers' run-ups. Dennis Lillee consulted a running coach to make sure he was accelerating effectively into the delivery stride. Others have followed suit, albeit somewhat late in their careers, as **MERV HUGHES** indicated:

> Being young you have a lot more on your mind than running style. This includes where you are going to bowl, what type of delivery and so on. Looking back now, the run-up, delivery and follow-through are the most important stages of bowling, with run-up the most important.

JOHN HARMER believes that a bowler is an 'athlete until the penultimate stride', and so correct running technique is mandatory. **BRIAN MCFADYEN** contends that bowlers need an efficient run-up so that when they get to the crease, they don't need to place enormous physical load on the body. As well as momentum, he believes the run-up should place the bowler in a balanced position at delivery. McFadyen warns that it is very difficult to alter the running technique of a 21-year-old, and suggests that most work should be done between 8 and 15 years of age.

The length of a pace bowler's run-up has varied throughout the ages, but essentially it should be as long as needed to generate optimum momentum while enabling the bowler to be strong through the crease. **DAMIEN FLEMING** remarked that, like most young fast bowlers of his time, he initially 'ran in like Dennis Lillee with a high bound in the penultimate stride'. Later in his career, he shortened his run-up from 28 paces to 15 and found that he maintained his pace, was taller at take off and release and had a shorter jump into the delivery, but most important, he felt more powerful and rhythmical.

EFFICIENT DELIVERY

John Harmer offered the following keys to achieving an effective body position in bowling:

- Leg stability with limited collapsing of the legs throughout the delivery
- Compactness of the arms so that all force is generated towards the target
- Alignment of all body parts inside the width of the bowler's shoulders (see figure 4.1)
- An injury-free technique

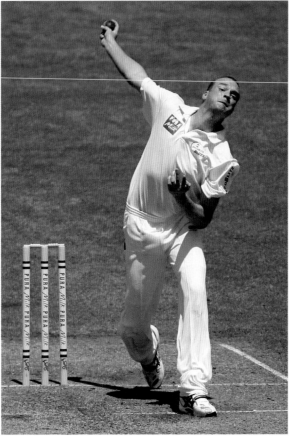

Figure 4.1   Stuart Clark in delivery stride with his feet aligned to his intended target and his front arm compact.

McFadyen also stressed the importance of alignment, explaining that the bowler's run-up and foot placement should be in a direct line to the target. **RICHARD DONE** cited the stability at back foot landing, but added that the direction of the front elbow and the position of the hand and body at release are important points in a delivery.

All of the preceding tips are relevant to all types of bowling from pace to spin. The following section presents specific issues relating to spin bowling.

Spin Bowling

Spin bowling is a complex art that requires guile, effective grips, strong body action and subtle changes in flight to deceive a batter. **ASHLEY MALLETT** identified the following principles in bowling spin:

- Ensure that the delivery action is supported by a strong, solid base.
- Stay tall through the crease, keeping the front leg straight and the leading arm high.
- Spend as much time on the front leg as possible, and use an up-and-over action to generate the energy required to spin the ball.
- The key is not where the ball lands, but how it arrives. The more time you spend on the front foot, the more purchase you will achieve on the ball. A hard-spun delivery with lots of overspin will cause the ball to dip acutely.
- If you spin the ball hard, you will have a bigger area of danger. For example, a Shane Warne leg break, shown in figure 4.2, achieves a danger area as big as a dining room table, but a more modestly spun delivery produces a danger area the size of a dinner plate.

- Off spin bowlers should keep their bowling arms higher than leg spinners do. In both cases, the front shoulder should point towards the target (to optimise rotation) and rotate like an upright wheel rather than sideways like a Frisbee.

A strong use of the leading, or non-bowling, arm has long been advocated for pace bowlers, but according to **TERRY JENNER** and Ashley Mallett, it is just as important for spin bowlers.

Swing Bowling

The ability to swing the ball in a traditional manner has declined in recent years as many bowlers, like Glenn McGrath, have favoured moving the ball off the seam. Many experts believe that this phase will change in the near future, as Harmer noted: 'Swing bowling will come back and is particularly suited in Twenty20 cricket. If the ball is straight, then you get very predictable and players are able to risk hitting through the line of the ball.'

Figure 4.2 Spin maestro Shane Warne at release of a leg break. Note the angle of the bowling arm to the vertical (approximately 20 degrees), the front elbow driven into his rib cage and the straight front leg.

Damien Fleming contends that the keys to orthodox outswing bowling involve positioning the wrist and fingers behind the ball with the ball angled towards the slips (see figure 4.3). With his wrist tilted to point the seam towards the slips, he imparted backspin on the ball as he slid his fingers down the seam at release. It was critical to maintain a stable seam throughout the flight path. Although some achieved this with two fingers close together, his preference was to have the fingers more apart (like Craig McDermott and Terry Alderman). Fleming also focused on placing his thumb right along the seam when he wanted to swing the ball. For cutters and slower balls, he recommended moving the thumb to one side of the seam.

Figure 4.3 Brett Lee demonstrating wrist tilt and finger position for traditional outswing delivery.

Fleming also noted that some bowlers, such as David Saker (former Victorian and Tasmanian outswing bowler), swung the ball effectively by pointing the seam towards slips but with their fingers pointing straight up the pitch at release. The key then appears to be to set the ball in the hands to maintain a stable seam position pointing towards the slips. The opposite action is true for inswing bowling: the seam points towards leg slip and the wrist tilts to accommodate that angle.

For reverse swing, Fleming noted two strategies that seem to work. Initially, players bowled with a rounded arm action to facilitate reverse inswing. Bowlers such as Lasith Malinga and Waqar Younis generated late reverse inswing with this method. However, Fleming noted that, in recent times, Victorian fast bowler Shane Harwood and emerging Indian pace bowler Ishant Sharma achieve reverse swing with the seam upright. This fairly recent phenomena in cricket needs further investigation and practice to determine the best method.

In all swing bowling, bowlers must shine the ball appropriately to facilitate variation in smoothness on either side of the ball. According to **CARL RACKEMANN**, the late Malcolm Marshall transformed pace bowling. With his front-on action, he was able, through positioning his wrist correctly, to bowl outswing as well as the traditional inswing that is typically achieved with this action.

The information in this section is not meant to be a comprehensive coverage of techniques in bowling. Rather, it is intended to address the basics of sound technique. Players need to be persistent and learn to bowl both traditional swing and reverse swing deliveries to maintain potency in their armoury.

Bowling Practices

Bowling is a closed skill, which means that its execution is totally dependent on the bowler's hitting a target area on the pitch. By contrast, batting, fielding and wicketkeeping are open skills, which means that players in these positions have to be able to respond to the ball delivered to them by another party; they must therefore have a flexible mindset as they ready themselves for action. Because it is a closed skill, bowling can be practiced with or without batters. It is also useful to practice parts of a delivery that are causing concern and then try to incorporate that change in the whole movement pattern. The following practices focus on activities that bowlers interviewed for this book have performed to develop their craft.

Training Practices

Terry Jenner believes that drills are required to progress in bowling, and for a long time players have been reluctant to spend enough time on specific drills to shape and finetune their skills. Richard Done favours the whole-part-whole method when conducting drills with bowlers. In this method the bowler practices the part causing most concern first in isolation and then incorporates it into the whole movement. The following practices can help players develop consistency and potency in their bowling.

DEVELOPING RUNNING STYLE FOR PACE BOWLERS

Cathryn Fitzpatrick commented that even though she was a good runner at school, her technique was ragged with her arms flailing across her body. She worked mainly with a strength and conditioning coach and kept referring to videos of her motion to check that her arms were swinging in line. McFadyen also uses the conditioning coach at the Cricket Australia Centre of Excellence to refine bowlers' running techniques. This is done more incidentally in the conditioning program rather than as a specific program. McFadyen also said that work on running technique can be done during warm-ups for training and matches.

BOWLING LEGAL DELIVERIES CONSISTENTLY

Long and triple jumpers in athletics have similar aims to bowlers in cricket: to hit a precise spot with their foot after completing a run-up to develop speed. However, these jumpers get only three attempts in competition; if they overstep the mark on each occasion, they are disqualified. No doubt this increases the importance of practicing precise run-ups that consistently allow them to take off behind or on the take-off board to initiate a legal jump.

Bowlers traditionally have been less concerned than jumpers about precision in their run-ups. In fact, if there is one thing that has consistently been tolerated and, indeed, overlooked at training, it is the bowling of no balls. Yet we still see matches in which bowlers take wickets on no balls. Quite simply, this is an indictment on our coaching profession and signifies a complete lack of discipline by the bowling fraternity in general. The first step in righting this problem is for bowlers to develop long jumpers' commitment to precision. Many players and coaches have identified tips to avoid bowling no balls.

John Harmer uses a succession of steps to demonstrate that the focus should be on the back foot landing rather than the front foot landing. He initially goes for a walk and drops a 20 cent piece on the ground and asks each bowler in turn to run in and land their front foot on the coin, which is very difficult to do. Then he asks them to land the back foot on the coin; most can do that quite easily. He then works with players on a seven-step approach, starting with the left foot, to again land on the coin with the back foot. Finally, he replaces the coin with a stump and says to the players, 'If you continually land your back foot here, then you will never bowl a no ball'.

Both Carl Rackemann and Cathryn Fitzpatrick also focused on the back foot landing and used the umpire as a guide for take-off into the delivery stride. Rackemann believes that such a focus brought everything back from the front crease and allowed him to bowl legal deliveries consistently.

Brian McFadyen indicated that at the Cricket Australia Centre of Excellence, they continue to have trouble with no balls in the training environment and have tried many approaches to eliminate this problem, with limited success. Physical punishment such as doing push-ups or running laps as a consequence for continually overstepping the line has been the most successful, but least favoured approach. The fact that such punishment works is an indictment on our bowlers. If they bowl more legal deliveries under threat of punishment, then it follows that in many cases this is a mental, rather than a technical, problem. Bowlers simply need to care more at training and commit to bowling legal deliveries every ball.

Another checkpoint for bowlers is the way they start their run-ups. This is invariably inconsistent. McFadyen advocates a starting position with both feet together, as Andrew Bichel and long jumpers tend to do. McFadyen has studied long jumpers and as a result has asked his bowlers to use only two run-ups—a full run-up and a modified one used purely for technique work. Once their run-ups have become automatic, he urges his bowlers to measure it with a measuring tape and use this distance every time they bowl. Mostly, however, pace bowlers tend to wheel around and try to hit a mark with one foot to signify the start of the run-up. Video footage has shown McFadyen that the part of the foot that hits the mark can be very inconsistent between deliveries, which places the bowler at more risk of overstepping the mark at delivery.

TIP Bowlers, like long jumpers, must avoid overstepping the mark and bowling illegal deliveries. This means carefully measuring their approach, practicing how to commence it in a consistent manner and, during the delivery stride, focusing on landing the back foot in the same place each time.

CHANGING TECHNIQUE IN DELIVERY STRIDE

Carl Rackemann, Cathryn Fitzpatrick and Merv Hughes all had actions that needed changing to prevent further injury. Rackemann recalls that he was taught a side-on action with his legs aligned to fine leg. He had a lot of back problems until he changed to a front-on action with his hips facing the target.

Fitzpatrick changed from a mixed to a front-on bowling action, as shown in figure 4.4, over a two-week period of intensive practice. She did a lot of physical and mental practice to ensure that her arms were following the right path to facilitate a front-on action. She also used the key phrase 'Get tall' to remind herself of the need for a high release point.

Figure 4.4 Cathryn Fitzpatrick loading up for a front-on delivery.

Hughes changed from a predominantly front-on action with his front foot splayed to the left and his front arm pointing towards third slip for a right-handed batter, to an action that produced movement away from the batter. In the early stages, he experienced a lot of back pain because he was trying to get his front shoulder around more, but he still splayed his front foot out (mixed action). He then tried running in from a slight angle so that he realigned his upper and lower body for the delivery and found that this eased the pain and allowed some movement off the seam towards the slips.

TIP To prevent lower back injuries, fast bowlers should avoid using a mixed bowling action in which the hips and shoulders are not aligned during the delivery stride. Workloads also need to be closely monitored so that they do not become excessive.

Professor **BRUCE ELLIOTT**, a sport biomechanist from the University of Western Australia, believes that a mixed bowling action, in which the hips and shoulders are not aligned during the delivery stride, is still a serious injury concern, particularly among younger pace bowlers. In his research he has found that, although there is always some non-alignment or counter-rotation, this can become very damaging if it is excessive. He has the following advice:

> Coaches should insist that young fast bowlers minimise counter-rotation of the shoulder alignment and avoid excessive hyper-extension of the spine during the delivery stride. This can be achieved either with a front-on or side-on action, as long as the counter-rotation of the shoulders is less than 30 degrees. As they mature, there are other issues that must be considered that increase the likelihood of using a mixed bowling action and incurring lower back injuries. These include over-bowling, poor physical preparation and fatigue.

FOCUSING ON LENGTH PRACTICE

Many bowlers have used targets to develop accuracy in length, but Rackemann and Fitzpatrick have used different practical approaches. Essentially, their singular method involves wanting the batter to play a particular shot. Rackemann wanted the ball hit to the off side, and he wanted players to play forward without being driven. Because conditions changed so much that the target area varied on different days, Fitzpatrick believes there is not much point in bowling to specific targets at training. She does not believe in looking at a spot, but many others have advocated this approach, so perhaps this is a matter of preference.

Harmer uses an inverted plough disc for spinners, which is between 2 and 3 metres wide. Ashley Mallett and John Buchanan use witches' hats to provide a target for bowlers. In addition, Damien Fleming had an interesting way of adjusting his vision when he wanted to vary his length. For a good length delivery, he focused on a sponsor's sign on the stumps (about three quarters of the way up the stumps). If the outcome was too full, he would direct his attention to a spot lower on the stumps. If he wanted to bowl a yorker, he would look at the off bail. For a bouncer, he would focus on the helmet of the batter and strive for a high release with more shoulder action in the delivery.

MAINTAINING ALIGNMENT

Markers and lines can be used to facilitate a run-up and follow-through that is in line with the target. Harmer favours bowling into a net with two ropes shoulder-width apart, as shown in figure 4.5. The idea is to bowl with a three-step approach, aiming to keep all body parts within the span of these ropes. Richard Done uses the concept of train tracks or a narrow corridor to encourage bowlers to align themselves towards the target throughout the run-up and delivery.

Figure 4.5   Bowler using vertical ropes to check the alignment of body parts.

Damien Fleming once observed on video that he was aligned to fine leg, causing him to swing the ball too early. He tended to jump in towards the stumps in his penultimate stride, which pushed his body towards fine leg. He worked on his running technique to try to remedy this problem and used lines on the pitch to check that he was running straight towards the target (figure 4.6 shows a straight run-up). In time, he straightened his approach and became more compact throughout his action.

Figure 4.6   A straight run-up facilitates a bowling action that is directed at the target.

USING STATIONARY DRILLS

Spin coaches Ashley Mallett and Terry Jenner are both advocates of performing bowling drills without a run-up. In many cases more threatening deliveries are executed in stationary drills, as shown in figure 4.7, because of the enhanced use of the body in this practice. Kneeling drills, as shown in figure 4.8, are recommended as a prelude to training and are designed to get the feel of each delivery while observing the seam position for each type of spin. For example, the seam position for a stock leg break should point towards first slip, whereas for a big leg spinner, the seam should point towards second slip. Mallett recommends that these kneeling drills be done side-on for leg spinners and front-on for orthodox or off spinners.

Both Mallett and Jenner also use standing drills to work on 'perfect release'. The standing bowl forces players to use hip and shoulder rotation while also encouraging more effective use of the front arm and back. Jenner also likes to use hand-to-hand drills, as shown in figure 4.9, which are ideal for providing the bowler immediate feedback on her hand position and also the seam position in flight. In a similar way, Harmer uses drills for swing bowlers in which they work on the release of the ball. He believes players need to understand how the ball feels at release and encourages players to do a lot of three-step and release drills. He urges his players to do 70 releases per day.

MAKING BOWLERS ACCOUNTABLE AT TRAINING

So often, bowlers in the practice net situation are not accountable for their deliveries. Most shots are hit into the net, and the outcome of these deliveries is unknown. Was the ball hit to the field, or did it get through and perhaps reach the boundary? Additionally, bowlers typically just run in and bowl with no one except the bowler aware of the intended line and length of the delivery. To address this issue, Merv Hughes had all bowlers in a net inform the others where their next delivery was aimed. Thus, all were accountable for every ball bowled. Coaches could increase accountability by asking bowlers to describe the specifics of each delivery in even more detail such as outlining the intended swing, spin or flight characteristics of each delivery. For example, a bowler might say, 'This delivery is going to be an outswing delivery aimed at middle stump on a full length at 90 per cent of full pace'. In this way the coaches can see how closely bowlers' outcomes are linked to their intentions.

TIP When bowlers are engaged in net practice, they should nominate where each ball is being directed. Making a commitment to line and length enables them to better challenge a batter who displays specific strengths and weaknesses in a match situation.

Figure 4.7 Standing drill to enhance the use of the body in delivery when using spin.

Figure 4.8 Kneeling drill used to practice different types of spin.

Figure 4.9 A young spinner practicing a hand-to-hand drill.

BOWLING IN A FATIGUED STATE

Although fatigued bowling has become a little unpopular in these times of controlled workloads for pace bowlers, the fact remains that players do have to bowl in a match when they are tired. It follows, then, that they should practice under fatigue conditions, as Hughes explains:

> At one stage I wasn't bowling well late in the day. So I specifically trained to bowl when I was fatigued. I would go to training, run for 5 kilometres, do a fielding session and then bowl with an old ball. Today, bowlers rarely get to bowl when they are fatigued and as a result are a risk to their team late in the day.

GUIDING THE LINE OF A DELIVERY

Jenner uses a drill in which bowlers direct the ball at different lines to create subtle changes for the batter and perhaps produce a false shot. For example, he suggests that a leg spinner bowl three lines—namely, middle stump, off stump and outside off stump. Marking lines on the wicket can help to facilitate bowling good line. These lines may vary according to batting types (such as left- and right-handers) and bowling types.

GETTING THE FEEL OF THE MOVEMENT

Richard Done recommends using drills in which bowlers close their eyes when they perform the bowling action required. He believes that this helps to develop the rhythm and feel of the motion. Watching videos of elite performers can also assist in this process. Bowlers should then recall the feeling before each delivery in practice and matches.

Spin bowling is a very complex art that often needs practicing in part form to rectify faults. For example, it may be appropriate to just work on utilizing the front arm more effectively. Alternatively, practicing a 'power' release from the hand may help to impart more spin on the ball. Following practice of the part that is causing concern, the bowler then tries to incorporate that change into the whole movement. Further spin bowling drills are outlined next.

Mirror Bowling

Facing a mirror and without a ball, players go through the movement required for each delivery in their repertoire. Players should try to make all delivery type similar in appearance to each other to increase their chances of deceiving a batter. They should progress from underarm deliveries, to horizontal arm, to side arm and eventually to bowling with the arm at 20 degrees from the vertical.

Bottle Drill

Players can use a bottle to get the feel for the required hand positions for leg break, top spinner and wrong'un. In this drill, shown in figure 4.10, the bottle is placed in the hand of the bowler with the bottle top pointing towards the batter to enhance the hand position for wrist spinners.

Figure 4.10   Leg spin delivery: *(a)* with a bottle and *(b)* without a bottle.

MODELLING A SKILLED PERFORMER

In this three-person drill, a demonstrator stands out in front of a learner. The coach stands behind the learner and manually puts the learner's hands into the exact positions performed by the demonstrator. This approach can be used for all bowling and even throwing actions. The idea is for the learner to see the demonstrator's performance and try to imitate the position of the demonstrator's body. The coach is present to guide the player into a more efficient position if the player can't do so through imitation alone (see figure 4.11).

Figure 4.11   Demonstrator, learner and coach performing a wrong'un delivery.

PROJECTING THE BALL UPWARDS TO CREATE FLIGHT

A high bar positioned about 5 metres in front of the bowler will ensure that the bowler projects the ball upwards after release (see figure 4.12). This bar can be either held by two players standing on chairs or wedged between the two side nets.

ENCOURAGING A HIGH ANGLE OF ENTRY

A small hurdle for the ball to get over just before landing will promote a more vertical angle of entry of the ball to the pitch (see figure 4.13). This encourages the bowler to deliver the ball with more flight, which has greater potential to deceive a batter than one bowled with a flatter trajectory.

Figure 4.12 Spinner bowling over a high bar positioned 5 metres in front of the bowling stumps.

Figure 4.13 A hurdle can promote a more vertical angle of entry to the pitch.

CHANGING PACE AND LENGTH

Coaches can change the pace and length in drills to help players prepare for different types of balls. Ashley Mallett believes that when varying the pace on a ball, it is preferable to release the ball at different points. When viewing the arm path from side-on, the ball should be released just before the vertical, on the vertical and just past the vertical to get required changes in pace and length. An early release will produce a slower speed, and a later release will produce a faster delivery. Increasing the speed of the arm makes the change of pace too predictable.

USING CUE WORDS

Using self-talk, or cue words, to emphasise key parts of the skill required can be a helpful practice for players. For example, 'Up' or 'Snap' (to indicate a snap of the wrists) might be useful cue words for a spin bowler to think of during her performance.

COUNTERING LOW ARM ACTION

A vertical stand can be used to inhibit low arm action if that is a concern. The stand should be made of flexible material that can be knocked without harming the bowler. It is positioned just in front of the stumps where the bowling arm comes through. The distance from the bowler to the stand should be close enough to facilitate an angle of 20 degrees from the vertical when viewed from behind the bowler. This angle is conducive to bowling leg spin with good bounce. If the arm is too low (round arm), then spin may be generated, but bounce will be low. If the bowler hits the stand with the bowling arm, then clearly the angle is more than the desired 20 degrees. Conversely, if the arm is too high (i.e., near the vertical), then higher bounce may be achieved, but at the expense of leg or side spin.

Most of the following practices can also be used by off or orthodox spinners. Mallett recommends practicing to spin the ball up with the front arm high and the shoulders rotated. A good checkpoint is to see if the bowling shoulder and target or front shoulder are aligned when the ball is released. Also, players should spend a lot of time on the front foot by driving through the crease.

Mallett believes that players should learn to bowl a flipper (backspin delivery). He said, 'The flipper is any spinner's ball. Traditionally, it is a leg spinner's delivery, but off spinners too should use it'. The flicking of the fingers, allied with greater arm speed (for this particular delivery) will help enormously in players' quest to add the flipper to their repertoire. Mallett also stated:

> If you can flick your fingers, you are well on the way to bowling the flipper. The ball is held between your thumb and either your middle finger or forefinger. Some find it easier to use both fore-

finger and middle finger. The ball is flicked backwards. It is really like flicking your fingers with the ball between the thumb and middle finger. It takes some time to get the knack. A good way of getting the feel is to flick the ball from your bowling hand to your other hand. If you hold your bowling arm straight and flick the flipper, you'll find getting the knack happens quite quickly.

It is important to note, however, that players should *not* try to bowl a flipper over 20 metres straight away. Once players get the knack and can flick the ball, with it spinning backwards, from hand to hand, then they should try bowling it over a short distance, say, 5 to 6 metres. Gradually they will gain the confidence to bowl it over the full length of the pitch. But they need to be patient.

Match Practices

The previous section provided details of how bowlers can address various issues at training. Clearly, when things don't go right for a bowler in a match, he must adjust his approach or technique. Some of these situations are presented in this section.

CONFRONTING ATTACKING BATTERS

When an opposing batter looked to be in aggressive mood, Fitzpatrick tried to upset the batter's footwork. If the batter was scoring off the front foot, Fitzpatrick would bowl a shorter length to get the batter moving back to play shots. Then she would bowl one on a fuller length to see if she could entice the batter to play a drive after first moving back.

The key, according to Harmer, is to change something, whether it be the line, pace or angle of approach (around the wicket). He favoured bowling slower rather than quicker so that the batter had to make an adjustment. The first step in Jenner's solution to this problem was to look at the field and see whether a change could minimise the carnage. Then he would look at changing the pace and angle. To work over a batter, a bowler has to keep him on strike, so field placings and control are critical factors. Jenner believed this was one of Warne's main strengths.

Bowlers need to adopt different processes based on the situations that they are facing. Hughes contends that if a batter is attacking the bowling when there is a lot of movement present, the bowler should just concentrate on consistently getting the ball in the right areas. Eventually, mistakes will occur. If the wicket is very good, then the bowler can either continue to attack or seek to dry up the scoring. Hughes favoured the latter approach by avoiding bowling to a player's strengths. Typically, he did much the same as Fitzpatrick mentioned earlier—he tried to identify whether he was being hurt by front or back foot shots and changed the length to alter the batter's footwork.

McFadyen divided the problem of attacking batters into emotional and tactical approaches. First, he believed a bowler had to regain emotional control. Being attacked usually takes the bowler out of his emotional comfort zone. Using breathing control or imagery, he should try to return to his ideal performance state. At that point he is ready to address the tactical situation. Essentially, McFadyen agreed with the previous suggestion that the bowler needs to change something to combat the attack. Changes to field, line, length or pace were some of the strategies McFadyen recommended.

EXPLOITING BATTERS' WEAKNESSES

Harmer believes bowlers should look for lack of stability and upset the batters with change of pace and width. He suggested 'stalking' batters by not overexposing one's 'killer ball'. McFadyen bowled a variety of balls early to gain information; then developed a plan based on this feedback. If, for example, a batter played from the crease and wasn't able to move quickly into a forward position, McFadyen's plan might involve bowling five shorter balls and then a quicker, straight, full delivery to get through the defence early.

The modern player, according to Rackemann, has the distinct advantage of using video footage of batters to identify weaknesses. Replaying strokes over and over at various speeds can facilitate much more effective analyses of batters' techniques.

CORRECTING BOWLING ERRORS

Between innings, Fitzpatrick would watch video footage of how batters had combated her bowling and then hatch a plan to change her approach. During the innings, Hughes accepted that there would be bad balls, so he just 'got on with it'. He spoke of a tactic employed by the Australian team when bowling to former English batter Graham Hick. In this plan the objective was to bowl 30 centimetres outside off stump to frustrate Hick. On a bad day, Jenner believes, the challenge is to stay on. Lack of patience is usually a problem for wrist spinners.

McFadyen contrasted his typical approach as a player with that as a coach. As a player he used to go through a physical checklist, but as a coach he is more inclined to look for emotional factors. Typically, when bowling, he would go through physical aspects of his technique: 'Am I strong at the crease? Is my wrist maintaining a good position through the delivery stride?' However, on reflection, he invariably identified stress as a cause of his poor bowling and therefore worked on relaxing and allowing himself to perform freely.

DEVELOPING BOWLING PARTNERSHIPS

In recent times, the partnership of Warne and McGrath for Australia, who are shown in figure 4.14, has proven to be a deadly cocktail for opposition batters. Hughes contends that this is a most underrated aspect of bowling strategy. If, for example, an outswing bowling partner is setting up a batter by concentrating on getting the batter on the back foot, then it may

Figure 4.14 Fast bowler Glenn McGrath and leg spinner Shane Warne formed a formidable bowling partnership.

be useful for the partner to join that plan. Eventually, the swing bowler will bowl one of fuller length moving away to entice a forward movement and hopefully a nick to the wicketkeeper. At other times one partner may be bowling tight so that the other partner can afford to be more attacking. Conversely, when one partner is getting hit, the other partner must be a little more defensive.

Mental Skills in Bowling

Because bowling is a closed skill, as mentioned previously, in a sense, bowling is easier to execute than batting. Bowlers usually bowl when ready and are in control of everything from the moment they start their run-up. They control their tension levels, run-up speeds and how they release the ball. Unfortunately, like putting in golf, the outcome doesn't always match the intent, because the mind can get in the way of smooth and accurate bowling performance. Therefore, mental skills are very important for bowlers to learn. Several bowlers interviewed for this book practice some useful mental skills.

- Merv Hughes adopted the well-accepted philosophy of 'controlling the controllables'. Things that were out of his control, such as the pitch or weather conditions, the batter's ability, his team's catching ability or umpire decisions were relegated to the deep recesses of his mind. Instead, he focused on getting himself ready to bowl each ball to the best of his ability, no matter what the situation in the match.

- Brian McFadyen claimed that Glenn McGrath often sang a song to himself while running in to bowl. Although a somewhat 'left field' strategy, this approach could have a couple of benefits to bowlers. First, it might help in developing the rhythm necessary for producing a fluent run-up and delivery. Second, it could relax the bowler and prevent any negative thoughts or tension from occurring in the bowling motion. Damien Fleming explained that McGrath could do this because he had planned his six deliveries ahead of time. By contrast, Fleming could not adopt this approach because he wanted a more flexible bowling plan. Hence, he needed a ball-by-ball analysis and plan for the next delivery. As if to perpetuate the myth about the lack of intelligence of fast bowlers, Fleming did admit that he often sang a song to himself while batting. Perhaps that explains some of the 'Jacksonesque' moves of Fleming with the willow in hand!

- Ashley Mallett always tried to start a practice session as if he were bowling in a match. He wanted to practice his first delivery so that he felt prepared for it when he had to start bowling in a match.

- Mallett also advised bowlers to never finish a practice session with a bad ball. He wanted to end a session feeling confident in his bowling even if he may not have had a great session.

- Damien Fleming worked hard for one year on visualising himself performing the skills. He had a video of himself bowling well and viewed this repeatedly before matches. He believed this produced good outcomes.

Summary

The practices adopted by bowlers to refine their skills have been designed to improve consistency, variety and penetration. Bowlers must be able to vary the pace, line and length of deliveries, as circumstances demand. This requires regular monitoring of technique and the willingness to make adjustments where necessary. These practices must also prepare bowlers to exploit the weaknesses of batters as well as correct any faults that have crept into the technical and mental aspects of their games. In summary, they must to be able to bowl the right ball at the right time. Above all, bowlers, particularly fast bowlers, need to do this without fear of injury. Efficient running and effective bowling techniques are essential parts of this process, and training practices must be designed to ensure this.

Following are some of the practice recommendations for fast bowlers included in this chapter:

- Focus on developing an efficient running technique to generate momentum through the bowling crease.

- Learn to accurately replicate the run-up through to the delivery stride to minimise the chance of bowling no balls.
- Avoid using a mixed bowling action, which increases the chances of lower back injury.

Following are some of the practice recommendations for spin bowlers:

- Use stationary bowling drills to encourage greater use of the body during the delivery action.
- Bowl at targets or lines placed on the pitch or over bars or hurdles to develop accuracy and improve trajectory.
- Learn the correct hand position for spinning the ball with mirror, bottle and three-person drills.

When preparing for matches, bowlers should do the following:

- Evaluate the technique and approach of opposition batters as part of the process of implementing a plan aimed at bringing about their dismissal.
- Analyse video footage of batters in action to better understand their individual strengths and weaknesses.
- Implement a self-correction process during play to identify whether problems are technical or mental and then act accordingly.
- Make a commitment to line and length to better challenge a batter who displays specific strengths and weaknesses in a match situation.

CHAPTER 5

Fielding

As cricket has become more professional and faster paced, the importance of having athletic, multi-skilled fielders in all positions has increased dramatically. In years gone by, teams carried players who could either bat or bowl well, but who were almost inert in the field. Today, with shorter versions of the game becoming more popular, it is apparent that fielding can significantly affect the outcome.

The need for more accomplished and versatile fielders has necessitated the development of drills to prepare them specifically for their roles. Developing specific fielding drills has been difficult because they challenge both the creativity of the coach and the traditions of the game. And cricket, perhaps more than any other game, is steeped in tradition! Many traditional drills have survived not because of their inherent value in preparing fielders for specific positions, but because they were used by previously successful teams.

With coaches becoming more educated about the science of training, there has been an influx of drills that have a much more specific purpose than merely handling the ball. Clearly any ball handling and throwing will help a cricketer, but providing specific activities that replicate match situations can inspire more motivated cutting edge practice. Being able to do this remains one of the most challenging aspects of a coach's work.

Many of the players interviewed for this book were involved in the game before the need for specific fielding drills became so widely accepted. Therefore, it is not surprising that their practices may not replicate the requirements of specific fielding positions. It is fair to say that many current coaches and players still don't embrace the challenge of providing specific fielding drills. They seem to either think it doesn't matter how they set up drills or lack the creativity to design them.

To further complicate the choice of appropriate fielding drills, coaches have to decide whether they want to use drills that enhance fitness as well as skill or to focus solely on the basics. The best way to incorporate a fitness component while optimising efficiency and maintaining interest is to conduct a variety of fun drills with small groups. Coaches should also consider that fielding drills can be used to develop team spirit.

Fielders need to spend a lot of time gaining control of the basics of fielding. Repetition of correct technique undoubtedly cements a skill and enhances players' ability to maintain it in the pressure of competition. Of equal importance in grooving a fielding skill is making sure that practice is specific to the game.

Whatever the purpose of a drill, it must be conducted with a high level of intensity. With these thoughts as a backdrop to this chapter, it is now time to examine some of the principles of fielding technique.

 In the modern game the quality of fielding is closely tied to team success. In each practice session the coach must provide ample time for all players to work on their catching, ground fielding and throwing skills.

Fielding Skills and Strategies

Cricket Australia has demonstrated its recognition of the importance of fielding skills by appointing American baseball coach **MIKE YOUNG** as the national fielding coach. With his knowledge of and coaching skills in baseball, he has been able to identify the key elements of fielding in cricket. He emphasises the need to watch the ball closely when catching, to use the split step for better balance and lateral movement in ground fielding and to throw over the top rather than across the body for accuracy.

Of paramount importance is the attitude the player brings to a day in the field. Fielding can be tedious, so enthusiasm and interest can quickly wane. Bob Simpson, Ian Redpath and Belinda Clark said they loved fielding, and it showed. Dean Jones said that he hated running, but hit a ball to him and he would run it down and throw it back forever. Ian Redpath believes that good fielders want the ball hit to them. Dean Jones even counted his possessions in the field, such was his desire to be a part of the action. Consistently repeating the activity under a broad range of conditions and levels of difficulty was the aim of **NEIL BUSZARD**. He liked to introduce competition into his drills so his motivation remained high.

 When skills are well developed, coaches should introduce competition into fielding drills to duplicate match intensity, create an enthusiastic practice environment and build team spirit.

Catching

The old saying that 'catches win matches', although very catchy, does present a rather simplistic view of a game of cricket. Nonetheless, it illustrates the importance of this aspect of the game. Because the majority of wickets fall to catches, it is paramount that players practice this skill extensively in a specific manner. Simpson, arguably the best slip fielder ever, outlined the following technical guidelines for the special craft of catching:

- Be relaxed and committed to perfect technique to give yourself the best chance to catch the ball.
- In the stance you should feel as if your arms are falling off your body. Your knees should be flexed with your weight on the inside of your feet to facilitate lateral movement.
- Stay on your feet as much as possible rather than dive for the ball.
- Try to catch everything in two hands when possible.
- Never take your hands to the ball—let it come to you.
- Turn with the ball rather than staying square on to path of the ball.

In addition, eye movement is critical in catching, and this may vary from position to position. In slips, Simpson recommends watching the ball

all the way and not focusing on the edge of the bat, as many have been taught. He believes this approach enables the catcher to better judge the pace of the ball.

Buszard had different approaches when fielding in his two specialist positions at gully and point. At gully early in his career, he typically watched the bat, but he later tracked the ball and tried to determine the length of the ball. If it was short, he would get in a set position ready for a rapid cut shot. Conversely, if it was full of length, he would look for a thick edge and be prepared to move forward or to the side while maintaining a low position.

Fielding at point, to spinners in particular, Buszard tended to watch the ball again and judge the length. A short delivery might precipitate a cut shot, so getting into a balanced set position with the ability to move laterally was of prime importance. If the ball was full, the likely shot here was a push into the off side, so all preparation was geared to moving forward quickly.

In all situations it is good practice to watch the rotation of the ball. Dean Jones used to do this in all his fielding practice to improve focus as well as enhance his ability to predict spin once the ball landed.

Throwing

Until recently, throwing technique has not been a major focus in cricket coaching. Players were either good throwers or not. Some would throw side arm, whereas others would push the ball like shot-putters. Weaker throwers were hidden in the field. Ian Redpath commented that as a result of his coaching experience he has a better throwing action now than he did when he was playing. We have learned a lot from baseball coaches about throwing technique. Former Helms Award baseballer and cricket coach, Neil Buszard, outlined the following keys to good throwing, as shown in figure 5.1:

- Make sure the wrist, elbow and shoulder are working in unison.
- Transfer weight onto the front foot.
- Rotate shoulders and hips so that they come around the body.
- Because the front arm is important to set up the throw, drive it into the rib cage as the throwing arm begins to move forward.
- Ideally, be balanced and in good alignment with the target. (However, at times the need for a quick release will override the need to be balanced in order to make a close run-out.)

Mike Young warns players of the potential for injury from throwing infrequently in a match and from attempting a quick release if they are off balance. He advises them to remain warmed up while they are in the field and, whenever possible, to throw from a stable base to enhance power and safety.

Figure 5.1 Proper throwing positioning with high elbow and a transfer of weight.

Ground Fielding

The ability to apply pressure on a batting team through the use of aggressive, quick and clean ground fielding has become a major part of the modern game. Bowlers talk of building pressure on batters by restricting their scoring options. With a supportive fielding team, runs can dry up and either create run-out opportunities or produce rash shots from the batters. The keys to pressure ground fielding can be summed up as follows (also, see figure 5.2 for an example of proper ground fielding technique):

- Attack the ball and aim to field the ball as early in its path as possible.
- Stay down low and aim to be stable when the ball is nearing your hands.
- Keep your eyes on the ball and let it come into your hands with a giving motion.
- Use quick feet to jump into a side-on position to enhance throwing power.
- Execute the throw with either a crow hop or from a quick-release, balanced position. This decision will depend on the length of the throw required or the need for quickness as opposed to maximum power.

Figure 5.2 Proper attacking ground fielding technique with the player staying down low while picking up the ball.

Fielding practice has traditionally been the domain of a dedicated few. Bowlers, in particular, have viewed fielding as the gap between bowling rather than an area of specialty. However, this has changed, and the modern cricketer is expected to be a multi-skilled athlete who can catch in a variety of positions and be seen as a weapon in the field. In general terms, most players we interviewed suggested that at least an hour of every training session should be devoted to fielding. Bob Simpson, one of the pioneers in stressing the importance of fielding, believes that players should never have a ball out of their hands at training sessions. Neil Buszard, who was brought up playing baseball during the off-season for cricket, argues that cricketers spend far too little time consolidating their throwing technique. He contends that to get better, fielders need to have a throwing session every second day.

Fielding Practices

All fielding activities should replicate the specific requirements of the game. They should also provide optimal levels of participation and keep players interested. The intensity of practice should overload the players while providing quality fielding work. **TREVOR PENNEY** offered the following basic principles to guide the conduct of fielding drills:

- Drill practice should focus on practicing skills rather than just completing the drill. Players should focus on correct technique throughout all fielding drills. See figure 5.3a for an example of a typical low-intensity catching practice.

- All practice should be at match intensity.

- Concentration and desire should be at an optimum. Often in club situations, fielding drills are conducted in a very casual manner with lots of unrelated chatter and ready positions that do not emphasise alertness of body and mind. See figure 5.3*b* for an example of a typical high-intensity catching practice.

- Emphasis should be on the fielder reacting and moving to the ball quickly, allowing time to get into a balanced position. This ensures that the base is set before a throw, stop or catch is made.

- It is wise to start with more technical drills and then progress to more competitive and specific drills.

- Small groups, as shown in figure 5.4, allow for maximum opportunity to practice the skills.

Figure 5.3 Typical catching practice drills: *(a)* a low-intensity drill with players catching in a semicircle and *(b)* a high-intensity drill with players catching one-on-one.

Figure 5.4 Small group fielding practice that ensures high intensity with maximum participation.

- In all forms of the game, there needs to be more attention placed on match-specific fielding during practice, as discussed previously.
- Fielders in the inner ring should practice closing in on the batters.

The following practices were most recommended by the players interviewed for this book. Adopting these approaches to training and using repetitive, high-intensity drilling should ensure that fielders have automatic responses under pressure situations in matches.

Catching Practices

Practice sessions should cater to several types of catches: slips catches, which come quickly from the edge of the bat; infield catches, which either pop up or are hit directly at a fielder within a short distance of the bat; and outfield catches, in which the ball spends a considerable amount of time in the air before being caught. Slips and infield catches require quick reflexes, and outfield catches depend on being able to judge the flight of the ball accurately. In all cases, the positioning and response of the hands when the ball arrives are prerequisites for success.

 Drills that challenge players motivate them to continue to practice at high intensity. Pitting players or groups against each other and recording outcomes can elevate the intensity of fielding drills.

STRETCHING THE FIELDER DURING PRACTICE

It is sometimes desirable to expose players to more pressure than they would experience in a match. Bob Simpson liked to be closer to the bat in practice than he did in a match. Also, he used to push the other slip fielders farther away than they would be in a match (Simpson was a noted first slip specialist). This enabled him to increase his width of catching and thus stretch his boundaries. Other players (Ian Redpath, Dean Jones and Belinda Clark) liked to have catches hit firmly to them from 5 metres just to sharpen their reflexes for either fielding or batting.

The intensity of catching drills can typically drop off particularly in the stock standard semicircle formation. With five, six or more players in a semicircle, the drill can quickly become a social outing for players with the ball hit with minimal power and fielders adopting straight-legged starting positions. Many players (Redpath, Simpson, Fitzpatrick and Melanie Jones) emphasised the importance of hitting the ball hard so that players become accustomed to full-blooded shots coming at them.

Neil Buszard noted that former Test player Keith Stackpole and former Victorian player John Scholes would work on a variety of catching structures to prepare for any situation in a match. They would have guys hitting at them from short distances and from medium range, with pace and directional changes. With balls hit to the side and straight at them, they made a point of practicing catching with two hands and one hand on either side. They took a variety of catches, and Buszard believes that was the key to preparing for any catch that may come their way in a match.

USING OTHER METHODS AND EQUIPMENT TO PRACTICE CATCHING

Many aids, such as other equipment or areas other than the flat side of the bat, and a variety of locations have been used to try to replicate the feel of catching a cricket ball in a match situation. Some of these are presented here:

- Slip fielding from a thrower positioned about 15 metres from the batter who tries to edge the ball with a horizontal bat to the slip cordon, as shown in figure 5.5. This requires a lot of skill from the batter and is limited to horizontal shots. Many slip catches come from a batter who is playing essentially with a vertical bat, as in front foot driving shots. Another problem in this drill is that it is very time inefficient. That is, a fielder may get only a few catches in a 15-minute session if the batter often miscues shots or throws are a little wayward. Having said that, it is the best drill so far invented for practicing fielding in the slips.

- Slip fielding format with a thrower as described previously, but using the back of the bat. Bob Simpson believes this gives the catcher variations in the pace of the incoming ball.

- Using a slips cradle or a Katchit board, shown in figure 5.6, creates various angles of deflection so that the fielder is constantly moving to catch a ball flying off at different angles. Bob Simpson loved catching using the slip cradle because doing so really taught him to watch the ball closely.

Figure 5.5 Positioning of players for practicing slip catches.

Figure 5.6 Using a Katchit board for reflex catching.

- Using a baseball bat, as shown in figure 5.7, to hit catches from a short distance. The curved edges of a baseball bat can create more consistent deflections than a cricket bat can and therefore can provide more catching opportunities in a given time.

Figure 5.7 Using a baseball bat for reflex catching.

- Catching balls either hit or thrown on a variety of surfaces such as at the beach on soft sand or on rubber gym mats. The hard surface of many grounds, particularly in drought-affected areas, makes practicing diving for catches very painful and dangerous. Beach sand (or indoor beach volleyball courts, if a beach isn't nearby) or rubber mats are excellent for developing the techniques of diving for the ball and rolling with the catch to make sure it doesn't fall from the hands at ground contact. Both also offer wonderful opportunities to develop sound catching techniques. Bob Simpson, like many other young cricketers, spent a lot of time at the beach with his brothers scooting the ball off the water. He believed that if he could catch a tennis ball, he could catch anything, because a tennis ball must be caught with a giving motion or it will rebound from your hands.

- Catching balls that rebound off a wall. Ian Healy became famous for throwing and catching a golf ball that rebounded from a wall. Dean Jones also used this technique to improve his catching skill. Sir Donald Bradman was, of course, famous for hitting a golf ball rebounding off a water tank with a cricket stump to enhance his eye–hand coordination.

- Using baseball batting gloves to protect the hands to increase the volume of catching practice. Mike Young advocated this technique on the basis of his experience in baseball.

- Using a tennis racquet to hit a tennis ball to a catcher, as shown in figure 5.8. A tennis ball hit with a racquet can generate enormous speed, which is excellent for practicing getting the hands into position quickly and also for practicing the giving motion mentioned previously. In addition, catching a tennis ball fired out from a ball machine can also generate a competitive and enthusiastic catching session. High catches can be similarly practiced using a baseball machine to shoot cricket or tennis balls into the outfield.

- Playing other sports can aid the development of fielding skills. Trevor Penney noted that one of the best South African fielders of all time, Colin Bland, played a number of sports before concentrating on cricket. Penney believed that participating in other sports in the formative years can help players develop athleticism and anticipation in the field. For example, Melanie Jones had a gymnastic background, which she believed helped her develop the confidence and control to dive for the ball. Bob Simpson also extolled the virtues of a multi-sport background in his preparation to become an accomplished all-round cricketer.

- Keeping drills can be used to enhance catching ability. Belinda Clark did a lot of work as a youngster with Australian wicketkeeper **CHRISTINA MATTHEWS**, which she found most beneficial.

- Blocked catches of various lengths. Similar to Stackpole and Scholes, Melanie Jones, an outstanding fielder, liked to have sets of 10 catches at high intensity from 10 metres and 30 metres and high balls so she had to run forward and back.

Figure 5.8 Using a tennis racquet and tennis ball for reflex catching.

- Melanie Jones also liked drills that helped her focus on decision making. The use of balls of two different colours to indicate either a one-handed catch (red ball) or a two-handed catch (white ball) tended to sharpen her focus.

 Playing other sports can enhance fundamental movement skills such as running, jumping, catching and throwing, all of which have application in fielding and can be harnessed to improve performance. This should be encouraged from a young age.

As mentioned in the beginning of the chapter, making catching drills specific remains the most significant challenge for coaches. Replicating the way a ball is hit to a player fielding in the slips is very difficult. Outfield catches are easier but still need attention. For example, rather than just hitting high balls to fielders, it is desirable to hit balls that replicate the strokes likely to produce outfield catches. Fine leg fielders should therefore catch balls from a hook shot, so they are catching a ball with similar spin to what they will experience in a match.

Players fielding in the covers need to practice catching balls hit with a slice on them to replicate balls driven in the air with side spin. Trevor Penney positions fielders at various locations on the boundary and hits fly balls to them at fine leg, third man mid wicket, and long off and on to prepare his fielders specifically for the match.

Ground Fielding and Throwing Practices

The great fielders like to stop the opposition's best shots, as Ian Redpath recalled: 'I fielded at point to Graeme Pollock in a Test in Durban and enjoyed the challenge of trying to cut off the many shots he played into that area during a long innings'. Initially, in developing fielding or throwing drills, coaches need to determine their purpose. Are they mostly concerned with the quality of technique? Are they interested in players taking risks to pick the ball up and release it as quickly as possible? Are they principally interested in the fitness component of a drill, or are they looking for a drill that provides some fun and team enthusiasm? Fielders need to strike a balance between fielding and throwing the ball quickly and getting set for the most powerful throw they can muster. Contrasting views were expressed on this issue to demonstrate the problem facing coaches and players.

Brian McFadyen has evolved an approach that tries to balance work on the basics with the variety needed for dealing with unpredictable situations in matches. Initially in his coaching, he developed a lot of drills that provided ball-handling and fitness work, but he didn't believe they focused on developing the core basic fielding skills now required for elite cricketers. Players executed the drills at a high level of intensity but often with poor technique. Now, McFadyen has his players spend 80 per cent of their time on the basics of gathering the ball and throwing from a stable position. The remaining time is spent on drills that catered to fun, fitness and team dynamics.

Although Neil Buszard understands and practices the basics of ground fielding and throwing, he recognises that cricket fielding is not the same as baseball fielding. In trying for a close run-out from the infield, cricket fielders don't get the chance to get balanced and throw in a technically correct power position. On these occasions, if they field the ball with two hands and then do a crow hop before releasing the ball, they will have no chance of completing a run-out. This situation calls for some risk taking; players have to attack the ball, field it on the run and let it go, sometimes off the wrong foot. Buszard contends that fielders need to practice picking up and throwing on the run to prepare for these eventualities.

Footwork in fielding is just as important as it is in batting and must be practiced. Rapid movement to the ball provides the best chance of making a run-out. Following are several footwork practices.

USING QUICK FEET

Neil Buszard liked using drills to practice quick feet and quick release from the infield. One drill in particular, described here, combined the three main aspects of ground fielding—namely, the aggressive run to pick up, quick feet to align to the target and a quick release. It also had a fitness component that enabled the fielder to practice under fatigue conditions similar to those experienced in a match. An advantage of this drill is that the coach doesn't have to be involved and can watch the practice.

In this drill, the ball is rolled firmly by player A over a distance of 20-30 metres from a set of stumps toward player B. Player B fields the ball with both hands and, using quick feet, realigns the body to a side-on, powerful position and throws to a wicketkeeper placed a similar distance away to one side. The wicketkeeper then rolls the ball back toward player B, who continues to move forward, then flicks it to player C, who is positioned to receive it at the stumps. The process begins again with player C rolling the ball to a fourth player. After taking a turn, each player proceeds to the position to which he or she delivered the ball.

The drill involves ground fielding, quick feet, throwing (from both the power position and on the run) and short flick throws. In addition, there is an element of fielding under physical pressure as fatigue sets in. When the drill is reversed (i.e., the ball is rolled from the opposite side), the fielding emphasis changes from 'quick feet and release' to 'pick up and throw on the run'. This drill is executed best with four to six players.

SLIDING FOR THE BALL

The technique for sliding, shown in figure 5.9, is a fairly recent introduction to a fielder's repertoire and should not be practiced by those whose joints are on the wane. It is clearly designed to enable a player to chase the ball, retrieve it and release it quickly with a powerful throw. Penney suggests limiting this technique to wet grass so the body can slip easily on the surface, thereby reducing the risk of injury.

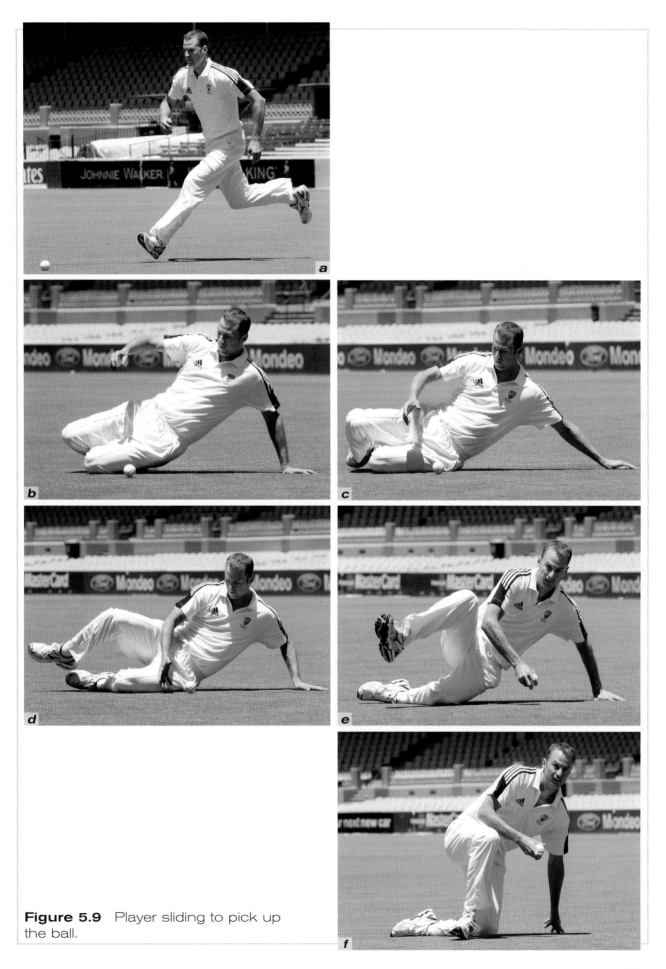

Figure 5.9 Player sliding to pick up the ball.

SPECIFICITY IN FIELDING

As in catching, ground fielding is best done with the hitter and fielders in position and the stumps set up as in a match situation so that the throwing distance and angle are more matchlike (see figure 5.10 for an example of player positioning for infield practice). Melanie Jones and Cathryn Fitzpatrick both prefer this format for their ground fielding practice. With this drill it is preferable to have no more than six fielders so there are plenty of opportunities for participation.

TEAM FITNESS DRILLS

Mike Young encourages a strong team approach to fielding, which includes what he refers to as 'wolf packing,' where a ball hit into the outfield is approached from three different angles. A pair of fielders chase the ball while a cut-off player moves to a position in the midfield to intercept a hard, flat throw from one of them and then returns the ball to either the keeper's or bowler's end, whichever provides the best chance of a run out. Players are encouraged to jog back to their fielding positions to maintain team tempo throughout the match.

Figure 5.10   Positioning of players for specific infield practice.

Figure 5.11 Goalkeeping drill set-up.

GOALKEEPING DRILL

Quite a few players recommended a drill that involved protecting an area similar to goalkeeping in football. As shown in figure 5.11, cones are placed about 7 metres apart and balls are hit into the gap with a fielder trying to stop the ball. This drill is very good for encouraging players to dive and extend the width of the area they can protect.

Summary

With the increase in popularity of limited over cricket, fielding has become an important part of the modern game. Players must now be athletic, particularly in terms of their running speed and acrobatic ability, and be able to catch and retrieve ground balls skilfully and throw accurately from any position on the field of play. Practices therefore need to involve both skill and fitness and should ultimately be performed at an intensity that is commensurate with the specific demands of the game. With this in mind, coaches must first emphasise technique and then ensure that the essential skills are performed at match intensity. They also need to be aware of the potential for the fielding practice environment to engender teamwork and generate enthusiasm among the players. Fielding drills therefore have a multitude of purposes, including fitness and team building, as well as providing the more obvious technical, position- and match-specific practice.

This chapter outlines the following guidelines in developing fielding practice sessions:

- Fielders must practice to be multi-skilled in slip and outfield catching, ground fielding and underarm and overarm throwing.
- All drills should demonstrate and reinforce sound technique in each of these areas.
- Technique work at less than optimum speed should be a continual focus throughout a fielding practice program.
- Unless working on pure technique, drills should be conducted at match intensity.
- Specificity in fielding drills enhances preparation for match performance and remains the most challenging aspect for coaches in preparing drills for training.
- A positive attitude to fielding is necessary at all times at training and in matches.
- Making drills competitive improves consistency and motivation.
- Small groups optimise practice time.
- Using other equipment such as a slip cradle, baseball bat, tennis racquet or golf ball can help develop catching skill. Catching practice on sand at the beach is useful for learning and consolidating the skill of diving for the ball.
- Sliding for the ball needs to be practiced, but it is best done on a slightly damp surface to minimise the risk of abrasions.
- Most drills should emphasise throwing from a stable base, but quickness and risk taking need to be practiced as well.

CHAPTER 6

Wicketkeeping

Wicketkeepers are very similar to umpires in that they are seldom noticed until they make a mistake. Why do we tend not to be aware of a wicketkeeper, when the role is so important in a team's performance in the field? Perhaps this is due to our focus. Coaches initially watch the bowler coming to the wicket hoping that there is a breakthrough with each delivery. Then they move their attention to the batter and the outcome of the delivery, noting any technical faults that perhaps can be exploited at another time. If the ball happens to pass through to the keeper, a coach might notice the keeper's position as the ball crashes into the gloves. However, coaches rarely focus on the important starting point and the movements made by the wicketkeeper into a catching position. For this reason they are seldom able to give keepers appropriate feedback.

And yet wicketkeepers are involved in a large number of dismissals through catches, stumpings and run-outs, and their role is likely to become even more important with the advent of Twenty20 cricket and its emphasis on fielding and depth in aggressive batting. Wicketkeepers also have a unique perspective on the pace, swing, cut and spin generated by each of the bowlers as well as the nature of the wicket itself. This makes them valuable sources of information for captains during matches.

> **TIP** When their team is fielding, wicketkeepers usually play a significant leadership role. They are in the best position to study and encourage the bowlers and become key players in fostering enthusiasm among the other fielders.

The renowned Australian wicketkeeper Ian Healy made the very pertinent, and indeed alarming, comment that most coaches don't know anything about the art of wicketkeeping. It is time to change this situation. In professional sports such as the various football codes and baseball, specialist coaches are appointed to attend to the needs of all players. Cricket must address this issue by appointing specialist keeping coaches to plan the preparation of keepers and evaluate their performance closely in matches. Coaches need to spend some time every match watching just the keeper, so they can provide meaningful feedback.

In the current climate, wicketkeepers are left largely to their own devices. Often, they band together and practice as a group, which can be beneficial. Wicketkeepers need to have an array of drills to prepare them for their demanding role. The repetition of drills that closely replicate the match situation as well as provide practice of the fundamentals is paramount to a keeper's preparation. As Healy remarked, 'I wanted to feel when I got into the game that I had been there a million times before'.

Before wicketkeeping can advance, coaches and players need to be more educated about the skills involved. As well, there is a mounting case for the appointment of specialist wicketkeeping coaches, when resources allow. We hope that the following examination of techniques and practices adopted by three well-respected exponents of the art—namely, **ROD MARSH**, Ian Healy and Christina Matthews—can contribute to the education of wicketkeepers and coaches.

Wicketkeeping Skills and Strategies

The art of wicketkeeping involves immense concentration and physical fitness. Although the skill set essentially revolves around the ability to catch a ball, it is in fact one of the most difficult skills to master. A wicketkeeper must be able to react quickly to late changes in the path of the ball and then move body and gloves rapidly and precisely to execute a successful catch. Rod Marsh maintains that the three basics of wicketkeeping involve the feet, the head and the hands:

> If you ever drop or misglove a ball, the reason will lie with these three fundamentals. In the ready position the stance should be comfortable and balanced with most of the weight on the balls of the feet. The head should be kept steady with the hands out in front. The feet must move quickly to get to the best catching position. An initial crossover step behind the body can facilitate greater lateral movement when standing back to pace bowlers. The head should be kept still at all times and be in line with the ball. The hands should point at 90 degrees (up or down) to the direction of the ball.

TIP Rod Marsh advises keepers to pretend that there is no batsman present and go through the process of taking every ball rather than watch the path of the shot after it is played. Practice should involve keeping on both sides of the wicket and to left- and right-handed batters.

Ian Healy believes that the body posture adopted when keeping up to the stumps is vital in achieving sideways power, as shown in figure 6.1. He focused on keeping his weight on the balls of his feet; his knees were bent halfway and his back was quite straight. Keeping his head over the gloves was also a priority.

Wicketkeepers must also develop the technique of diving for a take. If the catch is low and to the right, Marsh recommends diving to take the ball in front of the body, landing on the right shoulder and rolling under it. If the catch is high and to the right, then the catch should be taken behind the body with the trunk rotating backwards so that the keeper lands on the left shoulder, as shown in figure 6.2 on page 111. The converse applies to catches to the left side. In all cases, the aim is to prevent the elbow from hitting the ground, causing the hand to open and the ball to be spilled.

Marsh's and Healy's approach is reinforced by their counterpart in the national women's team, Christina Matthews, who modelled her practice on the attributes of these two players. She included diving and agility drills in her preparation to emulate the acrobatic skills of Marsh and realised the importance of having a stable base and rotating the trunk to the left or right sides.

Figure 6.1   Key points in keeping up to the stumps as exhibited by Ian Healy.

Wicketkeeping Practices

The aim of wicketkeeping practices for Healy was to learn to be in a good position to receive the ball and to be confident and relaxed with his glove work. He believed in simplicity with repetition and did not need much variety in the way he practiced. Marsh emphasised the need for perfect practice and stressed the importance of practicing to both left- and right-handed batters. He also advocated pretending to take every ball rather than watching the path of a shot after it is played. Most keepers work on keeping their reflexes sharp because they are constantly challenged to react quickly.

ENHANCING REFLEX CATCHING

Both Healy and Marsh liked to work on their reflexes to ensure that they could react quickly to a moving ball. Healy preferred short, sharp catches hit from 3 to 5 metres with the face of the bat, to make sure he wasn't snatching at the ball. He would focus on watching the ball, with the gloves and head going with it to absorb the force of the incoming ball. He would also concentrate on glove work, footwork and taking the ball inside the

Figure 6.2 Young wicketkeeper learning to take a high ball with a dive to the right side with the intention of rolling onto the left shoulder.

111

body. If one of his skills was not working, he would concentrate on that for a while. Ultimately, in each session he wanted to get to the point at which he could catch without concentrating on any technical aspect. During practice sessions Marsh used to take catches behind the wicket hit from a bat with a plastic edge attached to better facilitate nicking the ball through to the keeper. Also, he liked to stand very close to a catching cradle and catch balls thrown underarm into it. Matthews liked working with a turf roller and found that rebounds from its surface best simulated catching a nick from the edge of a bat. Others have used a cricket stump to generate nicks for wicketkeeping practice, as shown in figure 6.3.

STANDING UP TO THE STUMPS

Wicketkeepers tend to adopt one of two starting positions depending on the pace of the bowler. For slower bowlers, keepers stay close to the stumps to create stumping opportunities, whereas for faster bowlers they tend to stand up to 20 metres back from the stumps so they have the best chance to catch any deflections from the bat.

Healy had three key phrases that he would say to himself at various times when he was keeping up to the stumps: 'Watch the ball', 'Move', and

Figure 6.3 Former wicketkeeper and present national coach Tim Nielsen using a plastic cricket stump to hit edges to a keeper during a practice session.

'Stay down'. In practice, Healy practiced keeping up to the stumps with a thrower and no batter, and also with a shadow batter who just stood in position but did not try to hit the ball. Marsh would practice horizontal movement to the off and leg sides by rotating the hips and allowing time for the hands to give when catching the ball. Marsh also advocated catching a ball thrown into rough ground located near the crease line in front of a single stump. This created variable bounce, and he focused on staying down until the ball had pitched.

Healy became famous for honing his skills by catching a golf ball thrown against a brick wall. He believed this practice saved his career many times. He would typically do this drill in the morning or when he believed he hadn't had enough practice. He could practice standing up and back and work on his footwork and body posture. Doing this for a long period also added a fitness component to the drill.

STANDING BACK FROM THE STUMPS

Knowing when to go for a catch and when to leave it for the slips is a vital part of wicketkeeping. Wherever possible, Healy would work with a cordon of slips fielders with a skilled batter attempting to nick balls fired at him from a skilled thrower. Marsh would also do a lot of work catching balls hit with the flat side of the bat, commencing over a distance of about 10 metres. Again, he stresses the need to glide the feet into position, keep the head very still and let the hands give. The keeper should imagine that both left- and right-handed batsmen are on strike, and the hitter should be encouraged to extend the keeper's limits.

However, in practices conducted with a batter hitting balls from a thrower, the bat is typically in a horizontal position at impact. This does not exactly simulate what it is like to catch a ball that is edged after a full-blooded drive shot when the bat is near vertical. A machine that delivers a ball precisely to hit the edge of a vertically swung bat may be required. This would be valuable for both wicketkeeping and slip fielding practice.

PARTICIPATING IN FIELDING DRILLS

It is also important for the keeper to join in regular fielding drills. This includes throwing accurately for run-outs. Marsh recommends running to either side of the standing position, discarding a glove and throwing at the stumps at either end of the wicket. Both Marsh and Healy practiced running up to the stumps to receive a ball hit to a fielder to effect a run-out. Marsh used to aim to receive the ball just before arriving at the stumps. Healy believed that balls hit square of the wicket needed most practice. Wicketkeeper practice should also involve catching high balls that are skied behind the wicket. An attempt should be made to impart spin to the ball as would occur in a match. All three keepers we interviewed believed they had an important role in generating positive team talk and enthusiasm both during practice sessions and matches.

TIP Wicketkeepers should not only practice reflex catching and stumping but also work with the other fielders to develop their sprinting speed and the skills involved in catching high balls and executing run-outs.

PRACTICING IN THE NETS WITH BATTERS AND BOWLERS

Wicketkeepers have been the forgotten partner in the design of practice facilities. Until recently, most practice facilities have allowed only a small area behind the stumps for keepers to practice their art. Most elite venues still do not allow for a keeper to stand back in a net situation. This needs to be corrected in the future.

Most keepers like to spend some of their training time in the nets. Ideally, the task can be made more realistic by having similar bowlers operating in the net, but often this is not possible. Healy would typically work for three batters at a time and then do a half hour with a shadow batter before going outside the nets for an hour to perform other catching practices as described previously. Matthews did not go into the nets until she felt comfortable with drill work in the open field, which constituted 90 per cent of her practice time. This included keeping to half volleys thrown from a metre, standing both up and back to three-quarter pitch throws and diving for 3-metre throws, all to both the left and right sides of her body.

Mental Skills in Wicketkeeping

Because of the nature of the game, a wicketkeeper can go for lengthy periods without having an opportunity to dismiss a batter. Hence, having the ability to concentrate is vital to keepers' success. Following are a few points that wicketkeepers should keep in mind:

- Marsh asserted that keepers must learn to concentrate during practice drills because they are dress rehearsals for matches. He suggested that keepers practice turning on their focus the moment the ball is thrown to a hitter and switching it off after they have caught the ball. They should take a deep breath to relax and then move back to the starting position and repeat the process. This equates to switching on their concentration as the bowler turns at the top of the mark and remaining focused until the ball is dead. At that point they should clear their minds and restart the process as the bowler turns to commence another approach to the wicket.

- Marsh contends that wicketkeepers should study the bowlers in their team at practice. Clearly, it is an advantage to keep to them in the nets, but most nets don't allow for keeping to pace bowlers. Marsh became accustomed to the relative speeds of pace bowlers and was aware of the variety of swing or cut they achieved. He would look for cues in their action that would enable him to predict the type of delivery they would bowl. He also found it important to be able to judge the type of bounce that there was in a pitch to determine how far back to stand. The same principle applies to spin bowlers, although it is perhaps even more essential to work on being able to pick their variations because the time from the ball pitching to reaching the gloves is typically less for spinners. Wicketkeepers need to know these variations and be able to judge how much turn they will extract from any given surface.

- Healy made some interesting observations about his thoughts and actions when he was keeping well compared to when he was in poor form. On a good day he believed he had a clear mind, from the moment he went into a half crouch very late. Then he stayed low and strong and was ready to power sideways if needed. By contrast, on a bad day he would often be distracted by his thoughts and worry about his technique. He would ask himself, 'Why am I moving better on the right side than on the left?' He would start focusing on footwork rather than the ball and perhaps worry about the gap between himself and the first slip.

- Christina Matthews believed that she worked as hard on the mental skills involved in wicketkeeping as she did on the physical skills. This included learning how to overcome any self-doubts, to stay alert and focus on each delivery and to visualise the successful accomplishment of imagined scenarios (positive imagery).

Summary

With the advent of more one-day and Twenty20 matches, the role of wicketkeepers has become an increasingly important one. As key members of the fielding team, keepers are required to have quick reflexes, be acrobatic and have well-developed catching and stumping skills. From their strategic vantage point behind the stumps, they are in an excellent position to provide the bowlers with feedback and encouragement and create enthusiasm among the fielding team. Therefore, they are expected to play a significant on-field leadership role. Furthermore, they need to have good batting skills to increase the depth of the team's batting line-up. In modern cricket, having a good wicketkeeper is essential for team success.

This chapter explores the world of wicketkeeping as seen by two of the greats of Australian men's cricket, Rod Marsh and Ian Healy, and former Australian women's keeper, Christina Matthews. Following is a summary of the key observations:

- Coaches traditionally are not as well versed in coaching wicketkeeping as they are in coaching other skills of the game. Specialist wicketkeeping coaches need to be developed and used.

- Wicketkeeping involves the feet, the head and the hands. The stance should be balanced with the weight on the balls of the feet; the feet should move laterally and allow the head to remain steady over the gloves and in line with the ball. The hands should always point up if the ball is taken above the chest and down if the ball is below chest height.

- Keepers need to practice diving to both their left and right sides to catch the ball. For catches of various heights, they must perfect rolling on different shoulders to prevent the elbow from hitting the ground and the ball spilling from their hands.

- Repetition of reflex catching drills to ensure satisfactory glove work and footwork should be the basis of wicketkeeping practice.

- Most wicketkeepers practice catching the ball hit by a batter with either the edge or the face of the bat. This distance can vary but should attempt to simulate match conditions wherever possible.

- Drills for keeping up to the stumps typically use a shadow batter who plays and misses the ball so that the keeper gets a lot of catching practice.

- As well as receiving from a variety of bowlers, keepers should also practice catching high balls and throws from the fielders to effect run-outs.

- Net practice gives the keeper the opportunity to become accustomed to bowlers' variety of delivery. In most situations this is done while keeping up to the stumps because most facilities limit the opportunities to practice while standing back.

- Effective individual practice can be done with either a cricket or a golf ball against a concrete or brick wall.

- Wicketkeepers need to practice switching their focus on and off to simulate match conditions.

- Wicketkeepers should study the team's bowlers closely both at practice and during matches to better predict the pace, trajectory and bounce of the ball being bowled.

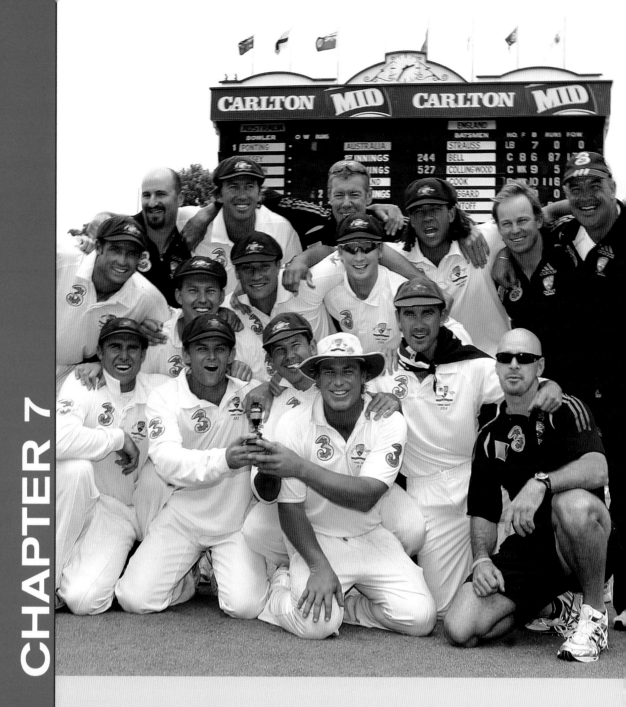

CHAPTER 7

Skill Practice Principles and Formats

This chapter firstly lists the principles that should be applied when planning practice sessions that will be effective in developing game skills. This is followed by a number of examples of practice formats which illustrate how these principles can be used to provide meaningful and valuable practice for batters and bowlers involved in all forms of the game.

PRACTICE PRINCIPLES

To prepare physically for the game, players should be individually and progressively overloaded with cricket-specific activities, yet have sufficient recovery between sessions. In addition to these principles of fitness training, coaches should factor the following considerations into a cricket skills training format.

Maximise Participation

Rather than have players standing around waiting their turns, coaches should subdivide the group to increase player involvement in the practice. This requires a well-structured session in which the intensity of the practice is high and players have more opportunities to practice their skills.

Maintain Pressure

The intensity of the practices should be sufficient to duplicate the pressure players are likely to experience in a match situation. In the initial stages of learning a skill, players should perform the activity at less than match tempo. However, as soon as practical, the pressure of the drills should increase to replicate the intensity experienced in a match.

Provide Variety

The interest and enthusiasm of the players should be maintained by varying the range of practices. Variety can be achieved by changing the structure of drills, using different equipment, altering the venue for training and practicing different skills. Sometimes, playing other sports provide worthwhile physical workouts. Variety can prevent the boredom that can occur with the constant repetition of activities.

TIP To provide a valuable practice session for players, the coach must identify the main purpose of the session and then ensure that its content and intensity are compatible with their specific needs.

Maintain Safety

During cricket practices, the safety of the players should be given high priority to minimise or prevent injury. Coaches needs to be armed with a number of ways of organising training sessions, and innovative coaches continually challenge themselves to generate more worthwhile training sessions. However, adhering to one principle may put players at odds with one another. Increasing the intensity and pressure of practice may test player health and safety. For example, overloading fast bowlers to prepare them for the arduous nature of their role in matches may conflict with the need to closely monitor their workloads and reduce the potential for injury.

Traditional cricket training involves the use of multiple nets with three or more bowlers competing against batters for periods of about 10 minutes. Clearly, this arrangement lacks both efficiency and specificity. Following is a list of ways to vary training to satisfy some of the preceding requirements.

PRACTICE FORMATS

The following practice formats utilise the preceding practice principles and are designed to prepare batters and bowlers to meet the demands of both the longer and shorter forms of the game.

THROW-DOWN ROTATIONS

In this practice, batters rotate through each net station and perform a predetermined skill for a designated period of time. Throwers are positioned at each net, but bowling machines can be used instead, if they are available. Skills performed at each net can vary from one session to another, but the practice structure remains the same. A six-net rotation with four turf nets and two hard wickets could include the following:

- *Net 1:* Front foot throw-downs including dancing to spinners
- *Net 2:* Back foot throw-downs
- *Net 3:* Normal net practice to three pace bowlers
- *Net 4:* Normal net practice to three spin bowlers
- *Net 5:* Hard wicket practice of evading bouncers using a golf ball to generate explosive bounce
- *Net 6:* Hard wicket batting against a ball machine (practice one shot)

It is important to rotate throwers or ball machine operators so that workloads are spread throughout the players and coaching staff. At any one time 18 people are occupied in essentially a self-managed practice—12 are participating in the practice, while 6 others are padded up for the next group of rotations. All other players need to be engaged in alternative fielding, skill or fitness work. Some advantages of this practice are that batters get more practice, and each bowling net is occupied by similar types of bowlers (i.e., spin bowlers do not operate in the same net as pace bowlers). Because bowlers are not required to bowl in each of the nets in any given practice session, the load imposed on them is lessened, which ensures that quality is maintained throughout the session and that batters receive systematic and comprehensive stroke preparation.

FIVE OVERS

In this practice, four bowlers are allocated to a net, each with one batter in it. Two bowlers of a similar type bowl five overs (30 deliveries) and then switch with the other two bowlers, who then bowl five overs. The two players who are not actively bowling, field in the nets and help to expedite ball retrieval to the active bowlers. After delivering a ball, bowlers return immediately to their marks to prepare to deliver another. The number of deliveries can vary from session to session depending on bowlers' needs. A useful variation is to have bowlers bowl six balls at a time to precisely simulate match requirements.

An advantage of this practice is that the time between deliveries for a bowler replicates that in a match. With four bowlers operating in a net, each bowler has to wait longer between deliveries than in a match, resulting in a practice intensity that is less than in competition. With two bowlers operating, there is less variance in bowling type for batters than if four bowlers were engaged at once. The coach just needs to try to pair bowlers with those of similar pace, spin and swing. Finally, there is more control over the amount of bowling completed at training. In traditional practices with up to 40 players working through four nets, coaches have difficulty closely monitoring the workloads of bowlers. Some enthusiastic, committed team players may feel obliged to bowl for over two hours non-stop. Such workloads are excessive and may result in either burnout or, worse, overuse injuries.

BOWLING CHANGE-UPS

In this practice, bowlers plan a set of six deliveries with five 'stock' balls and one 'change-up' ball, and then deliver that 'six pack' to a batter. The bowler can choose to vary pace, line, flight, length, swing, movement off the pitch or position on the crease. If the changeup delivery does not meet the expectations of the bowler, it should be repeated until a satisfactory outcome occurs. This structure is best initiated as part of a session rather than for the whole session, because bowlers need to practice for their own purposes as well. An advantage of this practice is that it provides a focus for bowlers and enables them to systematically practice a variety of appropriate changes to their stock deliveries.

ACCOUNTABLE BATTING

In this practice, two batters are allocated to a net for a minimum of 20 minutes. Bowlers then bowl to the first batter for up to five minutes in their first stint at the crease. However, if they are given out by a designated umpire (a player or assistant standing in the normal umpiring position at the bowler's end), then they are replaced immediately by the other batter. The second batter then has a five-minute opportunity to bat. If the second batter is dismissed within that time frame, that batter is replaced by the first batter and so on. The bowlers in the net are responsible for timing each five-minute turn at bat.

This practice should be used intermittently to remind players to bat with the same focus as in a match. The problem with using this arrangement at every training session is that the poorer players who need more practice will probably be dismissed more often and therefore get less batting practice. An advantage of this practice, however, is that batters place more value on their wicket, which simulates the match situation. Although some experimentation at training is good, batters should never adopt a totally carefree approach.

LIMITED OVER MATCH PREPARATION

At all levels of cricket, the nature of the game changes from week to week. Typically, a one-day structure is coupled with a longer version; recently, the Twenty20 format with its non-stop action has been added. Traditionally, training has tended to focus on preparing for the longer version of the game, but it has become increasingly obvious that preparation should be game-style specific. Here is a specific approach that might be used for limited over matches:

Bowling

Bowlers must practice bowling the width that is legal in the limited over format, so umpires should be positioned in each net to make sure they call wide balls. The aim of a bowler in a limited over match is essentially containment with variation of pace advocated more than huge sideways movement. Pace bowlers should work on bowling full-length deliveries that make it difficult for batters to get under the ball and loft it into the deep. Spinners should still be aiming to get wickets but should be bowling to minimise balls that could be hit to the boundary. This might often mean bowling with a slightly flatter trajectory and faster pace, although that may vary from batter to batter. Whatever the plan, bowlers should practice deliveries that are more likely to be needed in the limited over format.

 Practice sessions should cater for the versatility now required by both batters and bowlers so they can succeed in both the longer and shorter forms of the game. Coaches must plan practice sessions carefully according to the schedule of matches.

Batting

Batting roles in limited over matches can vary considerably depending on the situation, so batters need to be adaptable. For the sake of simplicity, it is useful to divide batters into two groups: high-order and middle-order batters. High-order batters should separate their batting time into the following three phases that approximate key phases in an innings, and middle-order batters should spend most of the time practicing phases 2 and 3:

- *Phase 1:* In the first phase, the field is placed in attacking positions closer to the batter to increase the chance of catches being taken and runs being saved, as for the start of the innings. Players should look to score singles and play aggressive shots when opportunities present themselves and occasionally try to hit lofted shots to clear the infield. A power shot should be followed by a search for a single to develop a sense of pacing an innings. Batters should still be willing to let balls go through to the keeper in this segment.

- *Phase 2:* In the second phase, the field has spread with four fielders permitted on the boundary. Such a field necessitates that the batter seek to score one or two off every ball. Maximum-power aerial shots are not recommended in this phase, but chipping over the infield short of the boundary fielders is an astute option.
- *Phase 3:* In the third and final phase, players practice innovative shots. Stepping away to hit the ball through the covers, moving inside the line of the ball to clip it over mid wicket and playing reverse sweeps are just some of the shots players should try in this segment.

SCENARIO BATTING AND BOWLING

Either in a net situation or, ideally, in centre wicket practice, players can be given various scenarios to carry out. These situations are limitless but should usually address what is commonly experienced in matches. Here are a few scenarios that illustrate this approach:

- The last five overs of a limited over match
- A target of 25 runs is set for the team to achieve within 30 deliveries (5 overs)
- Survival batting in which the batters have to bat for 20 minutes without getting out
- Bowling purely for containment, where the prime objective for the bowler is to limit scoring opportunities for the batters
- Scoring with singles only to emphasise working on shots that rotate the strike
- Playing one high-risk shot per over

HITTING TO SPECIFIC AREAS

With the advent of Twenty20 cricket, batters have to be able to hit the ball to areas of the ground patrolled by the fewest fielders, regardless of where the ball is pitched. In this practice a person (preferably an assistant coach or a parent) stands behind the bowler with different-coloured cards. A red card indicates that the ball must be hit to the off side; a green card calls for a ball to be placed for a smartly run single; an orange card requires producing a shot over the infield; and a blue card means that the batter has to dance down the wicket and clip it down the ground. If a bowling machine is being used, different-coloured balls can be delivered to fulfil the same purpose.

The preceding practices are just some of the approaches adopted by coaches as they seek to adapt to the ever-changing demands of the game and the players. Cricket leaders are constantly looking to develop practices that challenge players to prepare better for competitive situations. Leadership without this skill may short-change the player of the future.

PART III

The Practice and Playing Environment

The information covered in part III is critical for ensuring that a systematic and modern approach to player development will result in team success. Although individual players must be fit and skilful and switched on mentally, the team culture will ultimately determine what the team is capable of achieving.

Being able to develop a winning culture also depends on strong team leadership and management, as addressed in chapter 8. Both the captain and the coach must understand their respective roles and responsibilities and be able to work together harmoniously. The chapter also addresses the attributes of successful team leaders and describes the means by which several captains and coaches have been able to develop these qualities.

A winning culture is established when members of the team collectively agree on core values and then make a commitment to live these values both on and off the playing field. The method used to reach this consensus is described in detail in chapter 9, with specific examples drawn from both men's and women's cricket teams.

Although cricket has been a little slower than many other sports to accept sport science and technology, these are now being used widely to facilitate player development and devise team strategies. Chapter 10 describes some of the computer-generated and video-based technologies used for this purpose, in addition to manually recorded information. Both can play a valuable role in improving individual and team performance.

Chapter 11 places cricket at the crossroads. The public is presently in the position of deciding whether to support the shorter forms of the game or the traditional longer version. Eventually its opinion will have an impact on the way the sport is presented, including match scheduling, player selection and development and the strategies employed by captains and coaches to win matches. However, as discussed in this chapter, the fundamental challenge for any sport is to attract a large pool of talented players who then receive the support required to succeed. This requires strong leaders who can oversee effective development programs within vibrant and positive environments.

CHAPTER 8

Team Leadership and Management

Historically, the cricket captain has always been the team leader, both on and off the field. However, over the past 20 years, the trend in international and domestic cricket has been to appoint more head coaches. Unlike most other team sports in which the coach has overall responsibility for team performance and the captain is more of a figurehead, in the sport of cricket, the roles are different. The captain plays a stronger leadership role in match tactics and player performance, whereas the head coach manages the team preparation and match analysis. In this respect, they both have leadership responsibilities and need to work together closely.

Working Together as Captain and Coach

Former Western Australian coach **DARYL FOSTER** said:

> The captain–coach relationship is a vital factor in the success of a cricket team. Both have the responsibility for leadership, and their partnership is a critical factor in the team's performance. They must come to an understanding of their respective roles. The communication channels must always be open, and they must develop mutual trust and respect. If both the captain and coach operate on the premise of what is best for the team, then their relationship and partnership will develop into a strong and successful one.

Captain

Generally, team captains are expected to model the team values and have a match plan and style of play. During a match they need to be able to make considered and good decisions and be positive and enthusiastic. Captains should work closely with coaches, encourage input from the players, provide them with feedback about their performances and, critically yet constructively, evaluate overall team performance.

On match day, the captain's specific responsibilities are as follows:

- Consult with the selectors to determine the best batting order to suit the playing conditions.
- Discuss field placements with each of the bowlers, ensuring that an over rate is maintained that allows sensible decisions to be made towards the end of an innings.
- Coordinate the warm-up and cool-down routines with the coach.

Comments made by three notable captains underline the importance they place on everyone—the captain, head coach and other players—working together to optimise team performance.

John Inverarity, who captained both Western Australia and South Australia in the Sheffield Shield competition in the 1970s and 1980s, said that he consulted regularly with senior players in the team to get as much information about the match as possible. He also involved the bowlers in setting the field to give them some ownership of the situation.

> Knowing that everyone responds to certain situations differently, I always tried to handle matters on an individual basis. Depending on the composition of the team and the state of the match, I was keen to ensure that everyone, including myself, was optimally motivated to perform at their best. This means that individual players should neither become too complacent nor too excited, which is always a challenge across a diverse group of people. This is central to becoming an effective leader.

For some of the time that Inverarity was captain, there was no coach involved, so he had the responsibility for both the practice and playing environment.

> Today I believe that it is important for the captain to remain as the on-field leader with the coach responsible for program planning, player preparation and practice sessions. However, they must work together closely in the best interests of team harmony and performance. The captain must always be the leader of the team and the wider group, including the support staff.

When Mark Taylor became Test captain in 1994, he had meetings with vice captain Ian Healy, coach Bob Simpson and each of the players.

> I used the net sessions to speak to each of the players. We also had pre-game meetings with the team to ensure that the players were part of the process and felt some ownership of it. It was important for me to get feedback from them and have them learning while they watched the game. They were very good players and it was all about communicating with them and, most importantly, listening to them . . . . I think that the coach, Bob Simpson, and I had a very good relationship. I wanted to play a more leading role in running the team than the previous captain, Alan Border, but it didn't stop Bob from doing what he did really well, helping players with their fielding skills. We used to bounce ideas off each other all the time.

Belinda Clark, who was captain of the Australian women's team from 1994 to 2005, believes that the role of the captain is to get everyone on the same page and then be consistent and accountable.

> I think that it is very hard for a captain to expect something of a group if she is not prepared to do it herself on and off the field. This involves keeping players tuned to team goals, not allowing them to get ahead of themselves or, alternatively, put their feet up. Some players need extra attention, and rather than just speak to them, my preference was to do something active to help them find a solution. It is very important that the captain and the coach have a good relationship, understand their respective roles and work together as a team.

TIP Good communication among the captain, coach and other players, based on mutual trust and respect, is an essential ingredient
in a successful cricket team. This requires all parties being able
to deliver and accept constructive feedback.

To be successful, captains must be thoughtful and decisive, be able to
understand and communicate with members of the team and be respected
by them. Inverarity described himself as an enterprising captain who, to
a large extent, relied on intuition and instinct:

> While I had a plan when the team took to the field, I was always
> trying to read the opposition. I took notice of the comfort level
> of opposition batsmen against certain bowlers, as well as how
> they played particular deliveries and coped with different field
> placements. I was also aware of the strategies being used by our
> own bowlers, as well as their comfort level when bowling to
> certain batsmen using particular field placements. For example,
> Bob Massie needed to feel protected by field placements before
> being comfortable enough to bowl a fuller length and allow the
> ball to swing.

Greg Chappell was a captain whose philosophy was to lead the game
rather than follow it:

> The best way to win games is to take wickets. This requires
> having the best bowling combinations in action and setting fields
> which not only suit each bowler's style but challenge the bat-
> ters who are at the crease. When it comes to making runs, it is
> important to have a balanced batting order enabling youth and
> experience, left- and right-handers, stroke players and 'grafters',
> and front foot and back foot players to be at the crease at any
> one time.

Chappell also sees set plays as an essential part of the future of the game,
particularly with the advent of Twenty20 cricket. He stated, 'Each bowler
will need to have three to five different types of deliveries which will be
preset so that every fielder knows what is being bowled'.

Taylor always preferred to take the bit between the teeth and give things
a go rather than let things drift along:

> At the end of the day there is nothing wrong with losing a game
> of cricket provided that you can walk away knowing that you
> have done everything you can to help the side win. You shouldn't
> walk away thinking, 'What if we had tried this?' . . . I think that
> captains are generally more defensive these days, mainly trying
> to save runs. I would prefer them to be more proactive. To me,
> this isn't taking risks. It is simply finding a way to win the game
> by creating an environment where the opposition feels that things
> are going to happen to them. It keeps them guessing.

Clark was another captain who was well known for her bold style of team leadership.

> My adventurous approach was probably influenced by the fact that I was leading a strong team. I tended to play at different tempos, attacking at one stage and retreating at others, so that the other team didn't get a chance to understand the reason for the change. I generally had a basic plan but was always prepared to move away from it if it became necessary.

Coach

With the emerging significance of head coaches, it is vital that the players and all involved in the development and performance of the team have a clear perspective of their roles. This is particularly the case with the captain, who is the on-field leader of the team.

Rod Marsh, who has been the head coach at both the Australian and English Cricket Academies, attributes the growth in significance of the role of the coach to the increase in the amount the players are required to play and train. He said:

> The head coach has become very much a people manager who is responsible for programming both the players and the support staff. The players get individual programs, and the game is now about developing each to his or her maximum.

The head coach at the Cricket Australia Centre of Excellence, Greg Chappell, also sees the coach as essentially a manager whose task is to prepare players for matches and assist them to reach their potential. He said:

> On game day the coach may provide the captain with advice at breaks in play and be a good sounding board, but essentially the captain is in charge. A good working relationship between the captain and the coach is essential.

Richard Done, the high performance manager at the International Cricket Council, agrees that the coach's role is to plan the program, think creatively, set goals and regularly review the process and the results. He stated:

> This requires everyone associated with the preparation of the team being on the same page and players having access to a training environment which provides them with the best possible support staff and facilities.

Further, Tom Moody, head coach of the Western Warriors in Perth and former head coach of Sri Lanka, believes that as more staff become involved in elite programs, the management responsibilities of the coach will become even greater. He also emphasises that the complementary roles of the captain and coach need to be harmonised, according to the style of the captain and the dynamics of the relationship.

A democratic captain may be more open to implementing any new ideas suggested by the coach. On the other hand, an autocratic one may require the coach to act as more of a calming influence among the playing group. Of course, the capability of the coach to play either of these roles depends on his or her own personality and experience. However, **JOHN BUCHANAN**, Australia's national coach from 1999 to 2007, insists that neither the captain nor the coach should operate in isolation. 'I had good working relationships with Steve Waugh, Adam Gilchrist and Ricky Ponting which were in the best interests of the team', said Buchanan. 'This was not the case when I was coaching at Middlesex and clashed repeatedly with the captain, Mark Ramprakash. This had a negative effect on the performance of the team'.

Daryl Foster believes that the coach needs to have a working knowledge of all areas of player development that have a critical impact on the success of the team. In addition to liaising with the captain, the coach needs to plan and implement individual player programs in the areas of fitness, technique and mental skills; access cricket-specific services in sport science and performance analysis technology; and ensure that the players' lives and lifestyles outside cricket are compatible with achieving high levels of performance.

Greg Shipperd, head coach of the Victorian Bushrangers in Melbourne, believes that in the future more staff will be involved in the scientific and medical areas, which will increase the program management responsibilities of the coach. John Harmer, former coach of the Australian women's team, also believes that the emphasis is now more on the individual and that science and technology are playing a much greater role in player development and team performance. Even in a group training session, Harmer used his sport science and teaching background to identify technique problems with individual players and then work closely with them to correct it. He said, 'Players only know what they know, not what they need. Coaches have to address what they need and challenge them to improve in these areas'.

Harmer believes in the importance of providing immediate feedback to the player. The availability of a screen in the practice area that can play back an action during the 10-second period after the action has occurred greatly assists this process. Harmer said, 'This is an area of modern technology which needs to be used more in cricket, or coaches will have to rely on their ability to analyse a fault as they see it, which increases the chance of players replicating errors'. Present Australian head coach Tim Nielsen also emphasises the importance of prescribing individual training programs:

> Understanding individual players' strengths and weaknesses, and how they play, is critical if you are going to achieve consistent individual performance and improvement in a team environment. If there are six batsmen in your group, each has his own technique and mindset that has led to success in the past. Tapping into this as a coach and planning their preparation to continu-

ally challenge them is vital to ensure that the focus is not just on today but also on tomorrow.

Identifying areas in which new skills are required and then introducing these skills in a practice environment allows 'emergency' players to fulfil different roles. This might include opening the batting at short notice or filling in for a player who becomes ill or is injured. The objective is to be able to do this with minimal impact on individual and team performance. A clear understanding of each player's game and where each of them can improve will allow this to happen with little disruption or panic. My coaching mantra is 'Aim to perfect the basics, allowing you to do the more difficult things better'.

Neil Buszard, former coach of talented young players at the Victorian Institute of Sport, believes that changes in the way the game is being played should be factored into the way players are coached:

Scores are now much higher in one-day games. Players hit the ball harder and are prepared to take risks using a wider range of shots. This has encouraged coaches to change their thinking about how to bat and, as a consequence, about how to bowl. We need to allow young players to develop their natural talent by encouraging some flair rather than holding them back from exploring what their capabilities might be. I don't think that we should just categorise players in a certain mould but rather build on their strengths and see what can be developed next. It is the coach's responsibility to get the best out of them and improve their performance each year.

However, Rod Marsh has some concerns about the present situation. 'Players are no longer required to think for themselves. Coaches are doing this for them', he said. 'Coaches can be drawn away from the basics of the game and become over-reliant on technology and theoretical concepts. They should understand that the answer to any problem with technique will always be found in the basics of that technique'. He added that 'coaches can waste their time trying to impress players with textbook jargon. Communication is a prerequisite for being a good coach. Players need to be able to understand what a coach is talking about'. Bob Simpson, Australia's first full-time professional coach, shared some of these views: 'There are too many fads, fashions and theories in coaching these days. All great coaches work on getting the fundamentals right. Any advice needs to allow for individual flair'.

Both Marsh and Simpson emphasised the need for coaches and sport scientists to simplify the technical language they use in discussions with players. However, this should never mean that they close their minds to areas in which advances might occur. Developing a good understanding of the scientific foundations of cricket is the responsibility of coaches and players alike.

Understanding Leadership and Management

Strong and effective leaders are an important component of team success. Those with aspirations to lead need to clearly understand the responsibilities involved and the approach they should take to best fulfil the role. This involves watching and learning from others who have become recognised as successful leaders. The general leadership responsibilities of both the captain and the coach are as follows:

- *Create a shared vision.* Paint the big picture; set clear goals.
- *Show the way.* Establish core values; lead by example.
- *Enable the others.* Communicate openly; empower others.
- *Challenge the process.* Cultivate learning; encourage innovation.
- *Fire the soul.* Ignite the passion; inspire others.
- *Assess the outcomes.* Evaluate honestly; make informed decisions.

Some of Australia's leading coaches have identified a number of key factors in effectively leading and coordinating a cricket program. Nielsen emphasised the importance of team building, communication, learning and enjoyment when he said:

> The understanding that teams win and individuals contribute to this success is critical to ensure that everyone understands that no one player is bigger than the group. We all have a responsibility to keep the collective aims at heart when searching for personal success. Communication is critical in all team environments. Being willing to talk through differences or clashes and assisting to keep the collective view at the forefront of each person's thinking is challenging. However, when it can be achieved, you have the perfect environment for team and individual success.
>
> All the experiences gained through life shape your leadership philosophy. Listening to those who are willing to talk and guide you and then having the confidence to act when required is of paramount importance when leading people. Playing the game, dealing with professional and personal issues, taking every opportunity to add to your skill base and being open to the idea that there is a better way to do things will make you better prepared for the next day's work.
>
> You should also regularly ask yourself, 'Is this going to be fun?' We need to make sure that the team environment is one in which the players want to be involved and that they look forward to the challenges ahead. We need to make sure that they are enjoying the opportunity to play our great game.

Rod Marsh likened leading a cricket team to leading a business organisation:

Being in charge of a high performance cricket program is really not much different from being in charge of a company. The same leadership and management principles apply. Things such as communication, organisation, people management and initiative are all important.

A good manager will get to know the members of the group and decide what needs to be done to get the best out of them. This involves self-review to work out where any of your own deficiencies lie and then taking appropriate measures to become the best manager for the group. It is important that the manager leads by example and is capable of assessing any deficiencies in the staff that could prevent the organisation achieving success.

The staff must have ownership of the model, and my method is to allow them to determine it. Some need to be guided in the right direction, and this is achieved a lot easier if they believe that they are being listened to rather than directed. If the staff needs to be educated to ensure that they follow the success model, then this must be a high priority. If they don't take the model on board, then new staff must be found. This, of course, can be a delicate exercise!

The best teams have individual and team game plans and are able to execute them in a simple fashion. They have faith in each other's ability and leave nothing to chance in their preparation. The secret to good coaching is to allow the team to operate in this manner.

Dene Hills is another high performance coach who encourages the players to establish and follow team rules.

You have to communicate openly with the players and provide an environment that puts the responsibility on them to improve themselves by following the plans and rules that they have been involved in establishing. It helps to have the right leaders among the playing group who understand their role, set the rules and operate within a pure honesty system. Everyone must be on the same page, but know their respective boundaries.

Other coaches use similar terms when describing the merits of developing good relationships with players. For example, Neil Buszard said, 'Coaching is about building relationships with players through showing care and gaining their trust. If you show them an ounce of care, you will get twice as much back. If you provide them with honest feedback, positive or negative, about their performance it helps build rapport and gains you their respect'. Greg Shipperd stated, 'The most important factors in coaching and managing a team are consistency, honesty and communication', and John Harmer noted, 'I saw my role as developing individuals within a team culture. It required having a different approach for each player, depending on their personality and game sense, while engendering a team ethic based on enjoyment, effort and harmony'.

Learning to be a leader can start from an early age and, in many ways, is a never-ending process. There will always be issues and situations that have to be confronted and resolved in the best interests of team harmony and performance. When Inverarity was growing up, he learned a lot about cricket from his father, Mervyn, who captained and was a regular member of the West Australian side.

> Because of my father's influence, I appeared to know more about the game than the other boys and became their first choice to be captain. It always seemed to come naturally to me, and I was fortunate to get plenty of leadership opportunities. I enjoyed having my hands on the levers.

> I was a fan of Richie Benaud, who was captain of Australia when I was 14 years old. He had a real presence on the field, was innovative and always willing to try something unusual. Barry Shephard also had a big influence on me as a combative and unyielding captain when I was playing under his leadership in the West Australian team.

Key Elements of Cohesive Teams

The following six words personify what is required within a team aiming to achieve on-field success. In essence, it comes down to everyone being prepared to work together.

Communication—open exchange of thoughts, opinions and information (e.g. the coach providing feedback to the players regarding their performance).

Collaboration—combining the expertise of all parties for the benefit of the team (e.g. the physiotherapist and strength and conditioning staff agreeing on an injury rehabilitation program).

Cooperation—working in unison to produce a positive outcome for the team (e.g. the captain and coach coming to an agreed position on their respective roles in team preparation and performance).

Coordination—forming a harmonious combination in the best interests of the team (e.g. encouraging complementary batting and bowling partnerships).

Consultation—being prepared to seek information and advice from others, both within and outside the team (e.g. the captain referring to the coach about on-field strategies).

Connection—developing strong links between members of the team (e.g. a common way of thinking and acting underlying a sense of team connectedness).

> My development as a leader occurred mostly on the job rather than as a result of any formal training. My advice to any player who aspires to be a captain is to always think as though you are the captain, whether you are watching or playing the game.

John Inverarity was not only widely regarded as one of the best captains in Australian cricket, but went on to become deputy head of Pembroke School in Adelaide for nine years and then headmaster of Hale School in Perth for 14 years. He said, 'There is no doubt that my experiences on the cricket field were very valuable for playing a leadership role in the education profession'.

Taylor, who captained New South Wales and Australia, learned a lot from his first-grade captain, Ross Turner.

> Ross captained the side extremely well, through his communication with the players and by listening to them. He was able to get the best out of us both individually and collectively. We all got on very well together and played good cricket, and it was no surprise that we won premierships. It was because of the environment in which we played, and Ross had a lot to do with that.

Belinda Clark first captained Australia when she was 23 years old and was the equal of any batter in world women's cricket. 'I had confidence in my playing ability', she said, 'so I never felt really compromised. I was looking for challenges, and the captaincy allowed me to be more active when we were in the field'.

Coaches also learn a lot from watching and listening to other coaches, not only within cricket but also within other sports. Chappell describes the game as one that is constantly evolving, particularly since the introduction of the Twenty20 format. He said, 'This demands that coaches keep reading and learning to add to their knowledge and provide the best possible preparation for the players'. Greg Shipperd regards himself as fortunate to have played for Western Australia when Daryl Foster was the head coach.

> Daryl ensured that the right process was in place for us to improve as individuals and as a team. He brought substance and knowledge to the program and raised the bar for us all. It was process, process, process! I also learned a lot from some of my teammates over the years, Dennis Lillee and Rod Marsh. They had a lot of good people qualities and were mentally tough and skilful.

> I love following the football in the Melbourne papers, reading how various coaches evaluate the performance of their teams and what needs to be done to improve it. One coach said that his team was all attack and no defence. I applied this equally to the Bushrangers at the time, and it needed to be addressed. You can learn a lot from performance evaluations in other sports, which apply equally to cricket.

Leaders and managers must learn to lead by listening to recognised leaders and watching them in action. This includes those involved not only in competitive sport but also in other pursuits where performance counts.

Nielsen credits his father as being his cricketing mentor since he was old enough to talk:

> He helped me learn to play and love the game so that I got out of bed each day looking forward to whatever challenge would arise. I have also been fortunate to have Greg Chappell and John Buchanan as leaders and mentors. Greg's knowledge and experience in all aspects of the game have given me a tremendous grounding in thinking from a different perspective. Many of my ideas of what works best technically for players have been shaped by discussions with Greg.
>
> John took my understanding of elite coaching to another level. His willingness to look outside the square, use modern technology and challenge traditional norms have had a big impact on me. Using every resource and giving players and staff a chance to try things, without fear of failure, is something that I now try to keep at the forefront of my mind. It is not always easy to do.
>
> Most importantly, both Greg and John have helped me understand that there is no right way for different people to learn and develop and that it is my responsibility to use everything and everyone possible to effect individual and collective improvement.

Hills was also greatly influenced by these same coaches, both when he was in Tasmania and later at the Cricket Australia Centre of Excellence.

> I have learned a lot from coaches like John Buchanan, who thinks outside the square and has the courage to try things, and from Greg Shipperd, who has a great capacity for hard work. Both are very good people managers. However, when you get the opportunity, you learn from experience.
>
> You need to know yourself, your philosophy and your standards and how you are going to deal with different players. This continues to evolve as you read more about successful people and speak to other cricket coaches and those in different sports. You can also attend courses on leadership and people management, time management, player welfare and public speaking, all of which are helpful in assisting you to grow as a coach.

Rod Marsh appreciates that every group of players will have unique needs and that the coach must be able to meet these needs. He advised that the capacity to do this can be enhanced by reading, attending seminars and courses, visiting other successful teams from different sports and, of course, listening and communicating.

Although Tom Moody has completed a level 4 elite coaching course conducted by the English Cricket Board, he believes that he has learned a lot about communication and management while being involved in various cricket environments as a captain and a coach, including discussions with umpires, leading players and outstanding captains such as Clive Lloyd.

Moody has also had numerous conversations with leading coaches in other sports, such as Ric Charlesworth from hockey and John Worsfold from Australian football, as well as with leaders in the business world, such as the late John Roberts and Nigel Satterley, when he was working in the construction industry. He describes his approach to being a leader as 'always endeavouring to show the way rather than be led by others'.

Neil Buszard, who was an outstanding baseball player, has experience in that sport as well as knowledge of high performance programs in many other sports. He noted, 'At the Victorian Institute of Sport I was fortunate to be surrounded by coaches from other sports and was able to exchange knowledge and experiences with them. We all learned something from each other'.

John Harmer also has a broad base of knowledge of other sports, which he has brought to cricket.

> I am always trying to get better. It is an inner challenge which excites me. I like to teach something every time that I coach and have learned a lot from other sports such as baseball and tennis, which I have tried to integrate into my coaching. My teaching background in physical education has been very useful in understanding the scientific foundations of movement.

The captains and coaches interviewed for this part of the book are all passionate about the game and strongly committed to helping players maximise their individual talent and, most important, the performance of the team. They know that having a clear direction, being well organised and decisive and communicating openly with the players and each other creates an environment of mutual trust and respect that offers the team a greater chance of success.

CHAPTER 9

Team Culture

The culture of a cricket team, its brand or trademark, should be well known and understood by all who have a close association with it. Although the players, coaches and support staff are the ones most in the spotlight, many others play a role in ensuring that the culture is geared to high performance.

Ultimately, everyone associated with the team must be on the same page and subscribe to the same set of values and behaviours. This includes all those directly involved with the preparation of players as well as many others concerned with the governance, management and administration of the organisation. Parents, friends, partners, sponsors and player managers also have a strong connection with player and team performance and should participate in the process of creating a winning culture. This involves identifying what is happening when the player and the team are at their best and ensuring that this happens frequently.

Dr. Sandy Gordon from the University of Western Australia has assisted several cricket organisations undertake the process of implementing a winning culture. He refers to a winning culture as one of transformational leadership that has at its core a shared vision of sustained high performance. Fulfilling this vision requires the organisation to have a fundamental reason for existing (its mission), a strategy for achieving its goals and a set of core values that everyone involved embraces. Although Sandy Gordon has experienced success with this approach in Sri Lankan, Western Australian and English County cricket, he believes that ultra conservatism often gets in the way of trying to establish a winning culture.

> I often hear that you will never change the way the game is played, particularly from those who sit on boards or are from 'old school' administration and management. While many of their views are based on ignorance, they can disrupt the process of finding a better way to make good things happen more often. The best way to overcome it is to have those with strong cricket backgrounds, who are committed to the process, convince others of its value.

The process that Gordon uses to create a winning culture first involves members of the team or organisation agreeing on the core values that they hold, both in life and in sport. This requires having them look in the mirror and ask confronting questions such as, 'What do you think other teams think of you?' And then, even more important, 'How do you want your team to be regarded?'

However, as Gordon says, having universal agreement on a set of values is not enough. Those values need to be, what he terms, 'behaviourised.' Everyone must 'walk the talk' and translate them into the process of achieving performance goals. Within the team, it is the role of the captain and the head coach to model the core values and align the attitudes and behaviours of the players to them (for more information, see chapter 8 beginning on page 125). This needs to occur in the training, on-field and off-field environments and should be revisited several times throughout the season. Captains and head coaches also need to evaluate the performances of individual players and the team when batting, bowling and fielding as well as in comparison to other teams in the competition. Other performance indicators might include the number of players selected in representative or national teams.

 To establish a winning culture, the players in the team must agree on its core values, align their behaviours to them, determine challenging but achievable performance goals and then diligently set about attaining them.

Agreeing on Core Values

The first step in establishing a winning culture is to pair players off and have them choose their top four or five values from a list. They then meet with other pairs of players until the whole group ultimately agrees on a core set of values that drive the process of working together.

This step in the process should commence when the players are introduced to the program, but reinforcement of the core values that have been agreed upon, as well as individual and team expectations, needs to occur at regular intervals throughout the playing season. This is best done at special induction sessions in which all those associated with the team are present. It is then followed up during the season at regular meetings of the playing squad, in which discussions are held and decisions made regarding the essential behaviours associated with winning performance. The aim is to develop not only good players but also good people who respect and support each other.

The culture of a successful team usually includes some of the following values. They are reflected in the behaviours exhibited by the players when they are both on and off the field.

- *Passion.* Players must be passionate about their preparation and practice; their batting, bowling and fielding in matches; working together as a team; and adopting a positive approach to winning.
- *Work ethic.* Bowlers must prepare themselves for long spells, batters for long innings and fielders for all possible fielding positions.
- *Teamwork.* Players must enthusiastically voice support for each other while the team is both batting and in the field.
- *Resilience.* Players must have the capacity to persevere when wickets are hard to get and be able to recover from setbacks, such a series of quick dismissals.
- *Continual learning.* Each player must pledge to improve a limitation in their game, such as throwing or running between wickets, throughout the season.
- *Healthy lifestyle.* Players must ensure that they get sufficient sleep before matches and that their fluid and food intake is compatible with high performance.

- *Self-discipline.* Players must display patience while batting, bowl to a match plan and maintain intensity and skill in the field.
- *Self-determination.* Players must take responsibility for their own preparation and performance.
- *Self-belief.* Players must believe in each other and the capability of the team to achieve success.

When one of the authors, Ken Davis, was coaching at the Geelong Cricket Club in Victoria, the team embraced six core values: self-discipline, teamwork, excellence, preparation, unwavering courage and passion. The first letter for each of the values formed the words *step up*. This was very appropriate because it states exactly what was required: the players were expected to step up. It may not always be possible to match a catchy slogan to the values, but doing so is very useful because players then have a guide to remember them. Stickers were also made and emblazoned around the club and on players' cars so that everyone was constantly reminded of the values. Davis applied a similar process with the Victorian women's team, Spirit. The first letters of each of the core values (self-discipline, preparation, integrity, resilience, initiative and team) form the word *spirit*.

> **TIP** The team should try to devise a catchy slogan from the words that reflect its core values. This provides everyone with an easy way to remember them and adds greatly to their impact.

Aligning Player Attitudes and Behaviours to Core Values

The next step in the process is to link specific cricket behaviours to the core values and thus bring relevance to them. The following is a list of expectations of the Geelong Cricket Club players as part of the process of ensuring that they adhered to their core values.

Self-Discipline

- When batting in two-day matches, we need to be *patient and work our way through pivotal times in the match*.
- We need batters to be self-disciplined enough to *bat for lengthy periods*.
- In difficult batting conditions we need the discipline to *adapt and score from high-risk shots*.
- We need the discipline to *increase our levels of fitness* to the point that we are never beaten, we never get out, we never bowl a loose ball and we never misfield because of a fitness weakness.
- We need the discipline to *wear down opposition* bowlers and fielders.
- We need the discipline to *bowl to our match plan* throughout the day.
- We need the discipline to *field with intensity and skill* at all times.

Teamwork

- We need to *constantly voice team support for our batters* from outside the playing arena.
- We need to *come together as a team at crucial stages of our batting*—for example, when the match is in the balance.
- We need to *think of the team score* before getting excited about our individual contributions.
- We need to *commit to digging deep after we have lost a wicket* to build another partnership.
- We need to *be ready to bowl* at any time in the match.
- We need to *be enthusiastic even if we are not performing well.*
- We need to *help other players even after we have been dismissed.*
- We need to *continually voice support for each other on the field of play.*
- As batting partners, we need to *understand our individual weaknesses and guide each other*—for example, through periods of concentration lapses.
- As batting partners, we need to push ourselves to *achieve small goals along the way.*

Excellence

- We need players to *continually set goals for higher levels of performance.* For example, if you have taken six wickets, you want seven. If you have made 30 runs, you want 40. If you've made 50 one week, you desperately want 100 the next. If you've taken a great catch, you want to make a run-out.

Preparation

- Bowlers need to be *prepared through practice* to bowl at least 20 quality overs in a day.
- Batters need to be fully *prepared when it's their turn to bat* and therefore must constantly keep active and visualise an effective start to their innings.
- Batters need to be prepared through practice to *bat for long periods of time.*
- Fielders need to be prepared for *specific fielding in all likely positions.*

Unwavering Courage

- Bowlers must have the courage to *bowl with thought and aggression even when they are tiring physically.*
- Bowlers must have the courage to *bounce back after a poor spell of bowling.*
- Batters must have the courage to *want to bat in difficult conditions.*
- Batters must have the courage to *get behind* a fast lifting delivery.

- Batters must have the courage to *hit the ball over the top* if the situation demands it.
- Fielders must have the courage to *dive for a ball with the same desperation* at any stage of a match.
- Every player must have the courage to *want to be the one* to turn the match in the team's favour.
- As a team, we must have *more courage than our opponents!*

Passion

- As a team we need to be *passionate about our self-discipline, our teamwork, our excellence, our preparation and our courage.*
- As a team we need to bombard the opposition with a *consistently passionate approach to the task of winning the club championship and the first eleven premiership.*

Evaluating Performance

The final step in setting up a cricket season is establishing challenging but achievable performance goals for both the team and the individual players and then evaluating whether they have been attained. An effective way to begin this process is to analyse the performances of the team in recent years. This requires not only evaluating the overall results but also analysing the data associated with the playing process such as batting run totals and averages; the number of wickets taken as well as bowling economy and strike rates; wicketkeeper batting; length of partnerships; and several other indices listed later in this section.

The purpose of establishing criteria to evaluate individual and team performance is to identify areas that need improvement and to provide feedback to the players. The following represent some of the benchmarks that are presently being used to do this. They may need to be adjusted according to the skill level of the players, the standard of the competition and the general playing conditions.

Batting

- Four batters to average more than 30 runs per innings
- The opening batting pair to average more than 25, with one player over 35 runs per innings; the wicketkeeper to average more than 20 runs per innings
- One batter to score 70 and another 50 runs every time the team bats
- Team to have no more than two wickets down after the first two hours of play

Bowling

- Two bowlers to take more than 30 wickets in the season
- Two bowlers to average fewer than 20 runs per wicket

- Two bowlers to have an economy rate of less than three runs per over
- Team to bowl the least number of no balls/wides in the competition
- Team to bowl 25 per cent of the overs without a run being scored

Fielding

- All catching attempts to be taken
- Fielding team to make two diving saves per innings
- All ground fielding to be taken cleanly in the hands

This chapter outlines the process involved in establishing the culture of a team that is intent on maximising its level of performance. This first involves having the players agree on the core values of the team. By understanding the attitudes and behaviours that are expected of them, the players must then live these values as part of the process of trying to meet their performance goals. The chapter lists some of the core values that are commonly espoused by elite cricket teams and describes the attitudes and behaviours expected of the players. The benchmark performances expected of batters, bowlers and fielders in successful teams are also indicated.

CHAPTER 10

Science and Technology

One of the significant factors associated with Australia's improved performance in international sport during the past two decades has been the use of science and technology in preparing athletes for competition. However, cricket has been slower than many other sports to do so. Former Australian coach John Buchanan, for example, comparing cricket to swimming, which makes full use of science, called cricket a 'dinosaur sport'. However, with the advent of high performance youth programs at the Cricket Australia Centre of Excellence, there has been a gradual trend towards embracing a more scientific approach and using modern technologies.

Science

Adopting a scientific, or systematic, approach involves understanding the demands of the game, evaluating the attributes of individual players and then prescribing a suitable training program for each of them. The key word in this context is *individual* because every player is unique, which makes group training programs appropriate only for some members of a squad.

Three factors determine the quality of cricket performance—physical fitness, technical and tactical skill and psychological attributes. The fitness factor is the focus of the sport physiologist, who has the task of evaluating the demands of batting, bowling and fielding in terms of endurance, strength, power and flexibility and then prescribing appropriate training programs for individual players. Technical skill is the domain of the sport biomechanist, who measures variables such as force, velocity, acceleration and power to ensure that the player is using the most effective and efficient movement techniques. So far, this area of sport science has been applied mostly to evaluating bowling actions.

Behavioural sport scientists cover three areas of cricket performance: learning correct technique; making quick and accurate decisions; and acquiring the mental skills required to manage anxiety, retain a positive mindset and concentrate for long periods. In association with each of these sciences, performance analysts use modern technology to track player movements and the outcomes of their batting, bowling and fielding efforts.

In a cricket environment, sport scientists need to work closely with each other and with other members of the support team, which includes the coaches, the medical staff, physio- and massage therapists, nutritionists and the strength and conditioning staff. Everyone involved in the process needs to carefully monitor the program prescribed for an individual player and the player's progress.

Consider, for example, a bowler who injures a shoulder. A physician is required to diagnose the condition and suggest a general approach to rehabilitation. The strength and conditioning staff and physio- and massage therapists then prescribe and supervise the specific program and evaluate the bowler's progress. The sport psychologist monitors the bowler's state of mind during the recovery period and assists with setting goals and maintaining mental strength. Each of these professionals should be kept informed of the player's progress.

A player who is overweight and therefore limited in terms of movement capabilities requires multiple interventions. A sport nutritionist should be consulted to prescribe dietary changes; the strength and conditioning staff, to coordinate an appropriate fitness program; and the coaching staff, to progressively increase the player's participation in skill-based activities. A sport psychologist should investigate any personal issues that may be contributing to the player's weight problem. Again, regular communication among these groups is essential to ensure that the player progresses without experiencing any setbacks. This avoids any confusion among members of the support team that can create unrest and, even more important, unsettle the player involved.

 The technical staff involved in player preparation and performance must communicate on a regular basis not only with the coach but also with each other. This ensures a coordinated approach to maximising the benefits of each player's training program.

Sport scientists involved with a cricket squad must be familiar with the skills and tactics of the game and its demands on the players. By the same token, cricket coaches should be aware of the potential contributions of sport scientists. Because sport science is now an important component of modern coach education programs, high performance coaches receive a solid grounding in each of its sub disciplines. However, language barriers must still be overcome by simplifying the language of science so that everyone involved in the player development process can understand its concepts.

Technology

A number of modern technologies are presently being used in cricket to provide feedback for the players and the coaching staff. Richard Done from the ICC is confident that technology will continue to increase in importance in the future.

> The more tools available to provide players with improved and relevant physical, skill and performance feedback, the better. This could include functional assessment of skill movement patterns, instant video replays of skill training and continually better analysis of match performance data. Modern technology will enable faster, more accurate assessment of faults in technique, a better understanding of patterns of play and the development of more specific training programs and match strategies.

Player Analysis

John Buchanan, who has always adopted a scientific approach to preparing the cricket athlete, provides an example. He said, 'Back in the late '90s and

2000, we evaluated the workloads of bowlers during matches using GPS attachments to record the distances they covered as well as their heart rates and blood lactate levels. It enabled us to prescribe their training and recovery programs more accurately and prevent injuries'.

GPS monitoring of player workloads is continuing at the Australian Institute of Sport and the Cricket Australia Centre of Excellence. Miniature smart sensor technology units are worn to monitor fatigue and recovery levels, particularly among the fast bowlers, and can be used to rotate their involvement in the match and enhance team performance. Sport scientists communicate to the coach the workloads being shouldered by the bowlers as well as their physiological and psychological responses to them. This enables coaches to ensure that individual bowlers are not being overworked to the stage at which fatigue is having a negative effect on both their own performance and that of the team.

In terms of skill analysis, sophisticated sensor mats are now used on the bowling crease, the pitch and the side and back walls of the nets to give bowlers performance feedback on the line, length, pace and bounce of their deliveries and batters on the number of runs they have scored against fielders placed in set positions. Research conducted at the Cricket Australia Centre of Excellence has involved batting and bowling skill tests. By placing cone targets at several fielding locations and awarding points for hitting accuracy against a variety of bowling speeds, sport scientists have been able to identify the strengths and limitations of batters. With bowlers, vertical grid targets have been placed on the pitch where the batter stands. High-speed cameras and a radar gun are used to evaluate the speed and accuracy of each ball bowled.

> **TIP** The modern computer-generated technology that is now available in cricket enables the comprehensive evaluation of player techniques and match strategies. Coaches need to be fully aware of its potential to ensure that their teams are on a level playing field with the opposition.

When comparisons have been made among international, first-class and non-first-class players, the international group of both batters and bowlers has demonstrated better performances. This is most notable when players are batting against higher bowling speeds and bowling at faster speeds. This clearly indicates the validity of the tests being used.

Modern technology has also been used extensively for improving anticipation skills so that batters can predict quickly and accurately what type of ball is being bowled. Bruce Abernethy provided the following descriptions of practices in which technology is used to enhance cricket skills.

NET-BASED PRACTICE

- Shadow batting (or wicketkeeping) from a position immediately behind the net, wearing occluding goggles, with vision systematically occluded at or before the point of release of the ball by the bowler

- In-net batting, wearing occluding goggles, against bowlers using a softer ball, with vision either randomly or systematically occluded at or before the point of release of the ball by the bowler

VIDEO-BASED PRACTICE

A team can develop a large video library of many bowlers with different delivery actions. A batter watches a video sequence of a ball being bowled and, via a remote control, the image is paused by the operator at a point prior to the release of the ball. The batter attempts to predict the type and length of delivery, or, if a coach is present to control the video, plays a shadow shot. After the prediction or the shadow shot, the image is unpaused to reveal the actual type and length of delivery. The skill can be progressed by pausing the video earlier and earlier in the bowling sequence This feedback is essential for the batter to learn the relationship between the bowler's movement pattern and the resultant delivery. Thousands of practice trials are required for effective anticipation training.

Abernethy also noted that the advantage of video-based training is that many trials can be completed individually, out of season, without the need for net facilities, other players or a coach. Bowlers need to create footage of their own bowling action from the batter's position to check the effectiveness of their attempts at disguise and deception. This footage would also be valuable for the team's wicketkeeper.

This type of research on player performance is expected to continue as the game demands more and more precision. Coaches need to keep up to date with this information to enhance the performances of cricketers at all levels of the game.

Match Analysis

In recent years, Buchanan has observed that match analysis has become more precise with recorded data and vision appearing simultaneously. 'Being able to analyse, with vision, the dismissals of each of the opposition batsmen for the past 10 years and demonstrate flaws in technique will assist the team to believe that it is well prepared for the match. It raises their confidence and makes a huge difference', said Buchanan.

He has also experienced differences among players in their receptiveness to the use of technology. 'Some of the older players prefer to keep it simple, but the younger ones, including those at the Cricket Australia Centre of Excellence, are more familiar with computer technology and are not as hesitant about using it', he said. 'We need to stay in touch with the younger generation. The receptiveness of the squad to match analysis depends on how information is presented to them and needs to be evaluated regularly'.

Wagon Wheel Analysis

However, irrespective of the level of the match, it is possible to compile information that is useful for players and coaches without sophisticated technologies. For example, diagrams of the cricket playing arena can be used to chart the areas in which a batter has made scoring shots. These are known as wagon wheels and can be created by hand. The process can, of course, be facilitated by computer software programs that are now available and use different-colour codes to indicate how many runs have been made from each scoring shot throughout an innings. This information can be used to evaluate both batter and bowler performance.

Following are some examples of how wagon wheels might be used to plan strategies against particular batters.

Case1: Matthew Hayden

Wagon wheels of scoring shots for Australian Test opener Matthew Hayden reveal that he often scores boundaries driving the ball in the air through mid off. Strategies that the fielding team could use to counter this are as follows:

- Push the mid off fielder back to the fence and concede one run. If it is a one-day match, this then opens up the third man fielding position for scoring opportunities in the early overs when fielding restrictions apply.
- Push the mid off back halfway to the fence, but still concede one run.
- Place a fielder 20 metres from the bat in Hayden's line of vision, daring him to loft the ball. (Teams competing against Australia in recent years have adopted this strategy and have appeared to have met with some success.)

Case 2: David Warner

Australian One-Day and Twenty20 opener David Warner regularly hits shorter balls from on or just outside the line of the stumps over mid on or mid wicket. Strategies that the fielding team could use to counter this are as follows:

- Have deep, wide, long on in place from the start and have another deep fielder at squarish third man. Fine leg would be placed in the circle.
- Bowl a fuller-length ball 30 centimetres outside off stump with slip fielders in place.
- Maybe bowl an occasional ball closer to the line of the stumps at pace or off pace to entice the batter to try hitting over long on.

Case 3: Lisa Sthalekar

The wagon wheel shows that, when she is batting, Australian all-rounder Lisa Sthalekar scores prolifically either square or behind square on both sides of the wicket. This includes playing fine sweep shots and deflecting the ball with late cuts or leg glances. She usually scores very few runs in front of the wicket. Strategies that could be used by the fielding team to counter this are as follows:

- Have a short third man and short fine leg in place.
- Position a fielder at backwards point to cover the cut shot. The fielder should be a little deeper than third man because the force of the shot will usually be different in each case.
- Move mid off and cover fielders squarer.
- Move mid on and mid wicket fielders squarer. This strategy will force Lisa to look for other avenues to get off strike and minimise the damage caused by deflections.

The preceding scenarios illustrate the process of developing plans for batters based on records of previous batting history via wagon wheels. The same approach can be used for bowlers. Wagon wheels recorded over time provide the captain with indications of where particular bowlers have been scored from predominantly. For example, a solution to this problem could be to alter the line or length of the bowler, change the field to plug the gap in the field where scoring is occurring or analyse which batters are causing concern and just work on blocking the scoring shots of those players.

Run Sheet Analysis

Run sheets can be used in a number of ways to assist team strategy and performance. They allow a comparison of the number of balls faced and runs scored by each of the batting partners, the effect that this has on the productivity of their respective innings and the overall impact on team performance. As far as bowlers are concerned, the scoring rate provides an indication of the discomfort level of batters and, when considered with the shots being played to certain types of deliveries, it becomes a valuable guide when deciding what type of delivery to bowl at various times. Following are some specific examples.

Case 1

A batter gets out playing a high-risk shot to a wide ball after scoring 20 off 50 balls while being denied the strike, with 42 of the last 60 balls being bowled to a partner. This occurred because the batter had scored off the first ball of the over twice in the last five overs and was off strike for the remainder of these overs. Furthermore, the batter's partner had scored no singles from the last 17 balls.

Recommendation: The partner should give more strike to the established batter by looking for more singles.

Case 2

Before getting out to an aggressive drive, a batter had scored 48 off 45 deliveries, including four boundaries in the last three overs. Despite scoring nine singles in the first 28 runs, no singles followed any of these boundaries.

Recommendation: The batter should be encouraged to follow a boundary with a single. Spending time down the other end reduces the likelihood of trying to score a boundary off every ball. Such pacing of an innings allows time for batters to reflect on their good form and make sure that they are concentrating fully when next on strike.

Case 3

A young batter, who is holding the hopes of the team in a Twenty20 match, is 40 not out and cruising when an aggressive partner is dismissed. Six wickets are now down with 30 runs needed in the last five overs. The new partner misses three balls in a row to end the over, leaving 30 runs to be scored from 27 balls. The batter doesn't score for the first three deliveries received and then tries to hit the next ball out of ground and is bowled.

Recommendation: The batter should try to keep cool and trust the ability to score at a run a ball rate by playing shots along the ground and looking for twos. When on strike, the batter's partner has the responsibility to get the bat on the ball.

Case 4

A bowler has been hit for boundaries in the last two balls of the last five overs. The previous two deliveries had been let go by the batter when the bowling line was 30 centimetres outside off stump. When the bowler straightened up the line to the middle stump, the batter drove the ball to the on-side boundary for four.

Recommendation: Bowlers should keep persisting with a perceived line of discomfort for batters. They should make batters come to their plan rather than coming to the batter's comfort zone.

Case 5

A bowler is hit for 10 boundaries during a 10 over spell in a one-day match to finish with two wickets for 55 runs.

Recommendation: The bowler should consider a number of factors, including the field position in which the boundaries are being scored, the foot movements of the batter and the pace and movement of the deliveries.

- If the majority of boundaries are being scored from drives, then the bowling is too full or the field is not protecting the drive.
- If the majority of boundaries are being scored square of the wicket on the off side, then the bowling is probably too short and wide. This makes a case for bowling a tighter line into the body or placing a fielder at deep point.
- If the majority of boundaries are being scored on the leg side, then the bowler should adjust the bowling line to be more off side. If the batter is making a forward movement first, then the bowler should try to bowl a shorter length to get the batter on the back foot. Alternatively, if the batter is making a backwards movement first, the bowler should try to bowl a fuller length.
- If the batter is scoring from a slower ball, then maybe it is not well disguised, or, if the boundaries occur when trying to bowl different swing or spin, then perhaps the line or length of this changeup delivery needs to be altered.

TIP Coaches should take advantage of the modern technologies that are presently available to analyse cricket skills and strategies. However, they should also use less sophisticated techniques based on their own creativity, an intimate knowledge of the game and a close study of the opposition.

In addition to some of the more sophisticated technologies, there are also special pieces of equipment that have been developed to assist players prepare for the game. More recently, bowlers have had access to balls which vary in shape and texture as a means of improving their understanding of how they move through the air. The reflexes of slips fielders and wicket-keepers are tested by odd-shaped balls which bounce at different angles as well as by rebound nets and slips cradle ramps. Modern coaches are also using foam faced bats to improve their hitting precision and power when conducting short catching and ground fielding practices.

Swing trainers and weighted bat sleeves are available to improve the footwork, technique and power of batters. Trampolines and rebound nets have been used recently by John Harmer to improve the balance and hand eye coordination of batters. According to Harmer, early indications are that these techniques produce dramatic improvement in these aspects of performance. More of these innovative aids will continue to be utilised by coaches as they seek greater variety and specificity in preparing players for competition.

There are also some clothing technologies that need to be utilised. It is recommended that players wear anti-DVT stockings to avoid the possibility of incurring blood clots during long-distance air travel. The same technology is also being applied in the manufacture of graded compression garments which are presently being used by athletes in a number of different sports. These garments facilitate the return of blood from the limbs to the heart and increase the supply of oxygen to the working muscles. Their purpose is to reduce the accumulation of lactic acid and fatigue, minimise residual muscle soreness and hasten short- and long-term recovery. The garments, which come in the form of shorts, socks, tops and full-length tights, have a useful role to play in the training, match play and recovery of cricketers.

This chapter shows some of the areas in which cricket has started to embrace a more scientific and systematic approach to player preparation and performance, including fitness, technical skill, decision making and mental skills. The use of field-based testing of players in both the practice and playing arenas has greatly helped coaches develop individualised player development programs. Although modern technology has provided some valuable tools to assist this process, less sophisticated analyses can also provide the coach with useful information to facilitate better individual performance and team strategies.

CHAPTER 11

Cricket in the Future

The trend towards more Twenty20 cricket reflects a societal shift. Being able to get a result in three hours fits the busy mindset and the evening entertainment schedule of the modern sport fan. This is shown by the large crowds and viewing audiences who watch these matches. Many of these spectators and viewers may be less savvy about the nuances of the game than the cricket traditionalists, but they enjoy the action and excitement. There is now a world Twenty20 tournament, a one-day or 50-over World Cup, and regular Test match series between the major cricketing nations. While becoming a Test cricketer is still the dream of most young players, the shorter forms of the game provide more opportunities for them to participate on the domestic and international stage. In many ways each format appeals to a different type of player and spectator.

The schedule of matches involving all forms of the game has become an extremely busy one, and in the best interests of player preservation, the commitments at the state, national and international levels need to be very carefully coordinated and managed. Otherwise, there is a serious risk that players will be exposed to injury and burnout. Clearly, officials, coaches and players all need to keep in mind some key evolving aspects of modern cricket.

Qualities of Players

The emergence of different forms of the game means that cricketers now need a more diverse range of skills. Although versatility, adaptability and the ability to perform under pressure are all valuable assets, players with a strong foundation of core cricket skills have a better chance of success in all forms of the game. As in most sports, the basics are forever important.

Batters need to have both defensive and attacking skills and a touch of invention. Although Test cricket provides the opportunity to bat for lengthy periods, the short batting time and smaller grounds used in Twenty20 cricket make hitting sixes an enticing option. Bowlers need to be accurate and able to swing and spin the ball at will to succeed in any version of the game. Test bowlers may be given time to settle into line and length, but it must happen early during the four overs permitted in Twenty20 cricket, or a match may be lost. In any form of the game, fielders need athleticism and an ability to catch, ground field and throw from any position. The age of players with limited mobility fielding permanently in the slips is long gone.

The versatility of players can also be extended to batters being capable of switch hitting, as occurs in baseball; wicketkeepers being handy bowlers, hence allowing an extra batter to be chosen in the team; and bowlers who are competent with both swing and spin. Essentially, the cricketer of the future must have a wider skill set.

Match Preparation and Strategies

Match preparation and strategies also need close attention in the future. Practices need to reflect the intensity of matches, by including shorter periods of high-intensity effort. As playing schedules become busier, coaches need to carefully consider the wear and tear on modern players, particularly bowlers. Video analysis of the performance of opposition players and teams is now readily available and should be used to establish strategies to combat their effectiveness. Set plays by the fielding team are an essential part of this process and should become common practice. Rather than waiting to see what happens in a match, teams should be trying to make it happen.

The increasing emphasis on player preparation and strategic planning for all forms of the game places a greater responsibility on the coach. Although, historically, the captain has been the cricket team leader, this role, as in most other team sports, may, in future, become that of the coach. This means that the coach would be responsible for both off-field preparation and on-field strategies and performance. This may seem to be a considerable load for one person, but it is no different to that presently experienced by many coaches in other team sports.

Venues, Facilities and Technology

Night limited over matches have become popular, and the time is not too far away when first-class matches and even Test matches will be played under lights. More grounds and practice facilities will therefore need to be equipped with adequate lighting for both playing and preparation. Ball manufacturers will have to produce white balls with the same qualities as red ones, which can maintain reasonable condition for 80 overs. In addition, more indoor venues and drop-in wickets will be used. This takes climatic conditions out of consideration and avoids having to delay play for extended periods, which can influence results.

Training centres should be designed to allow practice in a confined mid-field area to minimise the need to retrieve balls that get past the players. So often practice situations are inefficient because players have to chase balls that get through the infield. With a field of approximately 30 metres on each side of the wicket, fielders could perform their primary infield roles without having to chase the ball to the boundary. At the base of the nets surrounding this 30-metre square area, a gutter could gather the balls and funnel them to a central point and thus eliminate the need to pick up balls. In this system player action would be very intense.

A similar ball retrieval system would allow batters to practice on their own in the nets, using a preset bowling machine to challenge their areas of weakness. The machine should be able to spin the ball as well as vary its speed. Cricket balls can eventually be designed for prolonged use in bowling machines. Plastic and rubber balls do not precisely replicate the flight path and bounce of cricket balls, so practice is not as specific as it might be.

As discussed in chapter 10, technology should also be available to provide both the player and the coach computer-generated feedback of the practice session. For example, technology should be developed to enable the bat to track the path of an approaching ball. The bat could be set so that the ball finds the edge of the blade and provides catching practice for wicketkeepers and slip fielders. Following the path of an externally-controlled bat that they are gripping could also assist batters to coordinate their footwork and move into the best position to execute efficient strokes.

No doubt other skills, technologies and approaches to training and match performance will emerge as the game continues to evolve. These changes will occur as coaches and players challenge the traditional approaches and explore new ways of preparation and methods of playing this great game.

Future Challenges for the Game

On a broader scale, cricket has many challenges ahead. Although the number of countries that are taking the game seriously has increased (and they are being assisted in this process by the International Cricket Council), there are concerns about the number and quality of players involved. Also, in the major cricket-playing nations, cricket competes for talent against many other sports such as professional football and those on the Olympic Games schedule.

In any country, the identification and encouragement of sporting talent is a fundamental concern. The talent pool must continue to expand, and the promotion of cricket among women, indigenous populations and immigrants should be given priority. This raises the issues of the calibre of school sport and physical education programs, the clarity of the talent pathways provided by clubs and associations and the quality and accessibility of talent development programs. Coach education through courses, seminars and workshops, as well as mentoring, is also an important component of talent development.

Cricket must also continue to break down its insularity and learn from other sports. Lessons from baseball and softball about switch hitting, set plays and fielding skills and strategies need to be further explored. Sports such as swimming, track and field athletics, gymnastics and hockey have much to teach cricketers about the use of science and technology; physical training methods; and fundamental movement skills such as running, jumping, tumbling and hitting.

These are but a few of our thoughts about the future of cricket. It is an evolving game, and what takes place tomorrow is limited only by our creativity. Significant challenges lie ahead, but no more so than in any other sport in the pursuit of excellence for the player, the team, the spectator and the wider community.

REFERENCES

Gucciardi, D.F., and S. Gordon. 2009. *The Cricket Mental Toughness Inventory (CMTI)*. Cricket Australia.

Gucciardi, D.F., and S. Gordon. 2009. Development and preliminary validation of the Cricket Mental Toughness Inventory (CMTI). *Journal of Sports Sciences*, 27, 1,293-1,310.

Gucciardi, D.F., S. Gordon, and J.A. Dimmock. 2009. Advancing mental toughness research and theory using personal construct psychology. *International Review of Sport and Exercise Psychology 2* (1), 54-72.

Lillee, D. 1998. Fast bowlers and the modern game. In *Wisden Cricketers' Almanack Australia*. Melbourne, Australia: Hardie Grant Books, 27-29.

Orchard, J., T. James, A. Kountouris, and M. Portus. 2008. Cricket Australia injury report 2008. *Sport Health 26* (4), 32-41.

Orchard, J., A. Kountouris, and T. James. 2007. Cricket Australia medical report India tour.

Winter, G. 1992. *The psychology of cricket: How to play the inner game of cricket*. Melbourne, Australia: Sun Books.

INDEX

Note: An *f* following a page number refers to a *figure*.

ABOUT THE AUTHORS

Authors Frank Pyke (*l*) and Ken Davis (*r*).

Frank Pyke has been involved in elite sport development as a sport scientist and administrator in Australia for more than 30 years. He played cricket at first grade district level in Western Australia, developed and supervised fast bowler Dennis Lillee's rehabilitation program following a back injury that threatened his career and coordinated the fitness programs for the Australian team in preparation for World Series Cricket during the late 1970s. Frank has also been the editor of all three editions of the textbooks for the National Coaching Accreditation Program in Australia in 1980, 1991 and 2001.

Following an academic career in several Australian Universities, he became the inaugural Executive Director of the Victorian Institute of Sport in Melbourne in 1990. He retired from full-time work in 2006 and is presently involved in teaching and facilitating courses in sport development, leadership and management in Universities and the sport industry. He holds a Masters Degree in Education from the University of Western Australia and a Ph.D. in the area of Exercise Physiology and Human Performance from Indiana University.

Ken Davis has played and coached cricket at first grade level in both Western Australia and Victoria for almost all of his life. Ken is a trained Physical Educator and therefore understands the needs of elite, youth and club cricketers. He also has a background in sport psychology which proved important in including sections of the text covering mental skills and preparation. He taught human movement and physical education at Deakin University in Geelong, Victoria, for more than 20 years, and he has worked for Cricket Victoria for the past 8 years and has coached both male and female cricketers.

Ken has a Masters Degree from the University of Western Australia that included a thesis on 'Fast Bowling in Cricket'. He also has a Ph.D. in Sport Psychology from Florida State University and is currently working as a Sport Science Consultant and is a member of the Cricket Coaches Association. He won the Coach of the Year award in 2005 through the Victorian Sports Awards.

ABOUT THE CONTRIBUTORS

Bruce Abernethy is a professor in the School of Human Movement Studies at the University of Queensland and concurrently the director and chair professor of the Institute of Human Performance at the University of Hong Kong. He played first-class cricket for Otago in New Zealand and first-grade cricket in Brisbane. His research, funded by Cricket Australia, involves the development of expert anticipation and decision- making skills.

John Buchanan played first-class cricket for Queensland as an opening batsman before coaching the team to two Sheffield Shield and two Mercantile Mutual Cup victories during the 1990s. Between 1999 and 2007 he completed an eight-year term as Australia's national coach, during which time the team won 68 of 89 Test matches and the 2003 and 2007 World Cups and clearly established itself as the best cricket team in the world.

Neil Buszard was an all-rounder who played in three premiership teams for the Carlton Club in Melbourne. He then coached Collingwood to another success in 1987/1988, before becoming head cricket coach at the Victorian Institute of Sport. He also represented Victoria and Australia in baseball and won the Helms Award as the best player in the national championships in 1974. He was a selector for the Victorian Sheffield Shield team from 1994 to 2002.

Greg Chappell MBE, was a higher-order batsman and medium-pace bowler who played in 87 Test matches for Australia, averaging 54 runs per innings, scoring 24 centuries, taking 47 wickets and captaining the team on 48 occasions. He also played in 74 One-Day Internationals and was a Wisden Cricketer of the Year in 1973. Following his retirement as a player in 1984, he coached South Australia in the interstate Sheffield Shield competition and the Indian national team and is presently head coach at the Cricket Australia Centre of Excellence in Brisbane.

Belinda Clark AM, was an outstanding batter and captain of the Australian team. During a 14-year international career between 1991 and 2005, she averaged 46 runs per innings in 15 Test matches and 47 runs per innings in 118 One-Day Internationals. In interstate matches she averaged over 50 runs per innings. She was a member of the teams that won the World Cup in 1997 and 2005, the latter as captain. She is presently the manager of Cricket Australia's Centre of Excellence in Brisbane.

Richard Done has been the high performance manager responsible for global development with the International Cricket Council in Dubai since 2004. After playing first-class cricket during the 1980s as a fast bowler for New South Wales, he has held the positions of senior coach at the Australian Cricket Academy and head coach of the cricket program at the Queensland Academy of Sport in Brisbane.

Bruce Elliott is a professor of biomechanics in the School of Sport Science, Exercise and Health, at the University of Western Australia. He has researched and published widely on the biomechanics of cricket, focusing on injury reduction and performance enhancement. He was the first to investigate back injuries in fast bowlers and, more recently, has been involved in modelling assessments to determine the legitimacy of bowling actions.

Cathryn Fitzpatrick was widely regarded as the fastest bowler in the modern era of women's international cricket. She took 60 wickets in Test matches and 180 wickets in One-Day Internationals during a 17-year career between 1991 and 2007. She was a member of the Australian teams that won the World Cup in 1997 and 2005. Upon her retirement as a player, she was appointed coach of Victorian Spirit in the interstate competition.

Damien Fleming was a swing bowler and valuable lower-order batsman who is the only player to have ever taken a hat trick on Test debut. He accomplished this against Pakistan in Rawalpindi in 1994. He played 20 Test matches for Australia, claiming 75 wickets at an average of 26 runs each, and took 134 wickets in 88 One-Day Internationals. Following his retirement, he coached at the Cricket Australia Centre of Excellence and more recently has become a radio and television commentator.

Daryl Foster commenced his cricket career in Melbourne before moving to Perth, where he guided Western Australia to nine Sheffield Shield victories and seven one-day titles between 1973 and 1995. He later coached Kent in the English County League. Formerly a senior lecturer in the Department of Human Movement and Exercise Science at the University of Western Australia, he is now a board member of Cricket Australia.

Sandy Gordon is a senior lecturer in sport psychology and sociology in the School of Sport Science, Exercise and Health, at the University of Western Australia. He has worked closely with several cricket teams and organisations in Western Australia, England (Hampshire), Sri Lanka and India, assisting them to develop a winning team culture and enhance the mental skills of the players.

Daniel Gucciardi completed an honours degree in psychology and a PhD in sport science at the University of Western Australia. His research was associated with mental toughness in Australian football, and he is presently working with junior clubs to enhance this component of performance in young players. His work has relevance across sports and has been published internationally.

John Harmer was a right-arm swing bowler and right-hand batsman who played and coached at the district level both in Melbourne and Perth. He lectured in physical education, coaching and biomechanics at Deakin University and was a popular presenter in coaching courses for many years before being appointed coach of the Australian women's team in 1994. After leading that team to three World Cup finals, he was appointed coach of the English women's team in 2001.

Ian Healy was Australia's wicketkeeper in 119 Test matches and 168 One-Day Internationals between 1988 and 1999. He was renowned for his exemplary glove work when keeping to leg spinner Shane Warne, for his 395 Test dismissals and for his performances with the bat, which netted him four Test centuries. He was a Wisden Cricketer of the Year in 1994, named as the wicketkeeper in the Australian Team of the 20th Century and is now a cricket television commentator.

Dene Hills was a top-order batsman for Tasmania who made 21 first-class centuries and three double centuries during a 10-year playing career. He was named the Sheffield Shield cricketer of the year in 1997/98. After retiring as a player, he became assistant coach of Tasmania before joining the coaching staff at the Cricket Australia Centre of Excellence. He was appointed a batting coach for the English team in 2009.

Merv Hughes was an aggressive and popular Victorian fast bowler who took 212 wickets in 53 Test matches between 1985 and 1994. He also took 38 wickets in One-Day Internationals and was a handy lower-order batsman. He was a Wisden Cricketer of the Year in 1994. After his retirement from first-class cricket, he continued to play with his district club, coached at the Victorian Institute of Sport and has been a national selector since 2005.

John Inverarity MBE, played in 223 first-class and six Test matches between 1962 and 1985. As a right-hand batsman who scored 26 centuries in first-class cricket and a left-arm orthodox spinner with best figures of 7/86, he captained both Western Australia and South Australia to a total of five victories in the interstate Sheffield Shield competition. He also had successful coaching stints with Kent and Warwickshire in the English County League.

Terry Jenner was a leg spin bowler who moved from Perth to Adelaide in 1967 and played in three winning South Australian Sheffield Shield teams. He represented Australia in nine Test matches and produced his best figures of 5/90 against the West Indies in the final Test of the 1972/73 series in Trinidad. He subsequently became a specialist spin bowling coach in several countries throughout the world.

Dean Jones AM, was a higher-order batsman who excelled in both Test and limited over cricket during an international career from 1984 to 1994. In 52 Tests he averaged 47 runs per innings, including his famous double century in trying conditions in India in 1986. He also averaged 45 runs per innings in 164 One-Day Internationals, where his athleticism and inventiveness made him one of the outstanding batsmen and fielders of his era. He was named a Wisden Cricketer of the Year in 1990.

Melanie Jones is a stylish right-hand batter and outstanding cover fielder who made a century in her Test debut against England in 1998 and has a Test average of 36 runs per innings. She was a member of the winning World Cup teams in 1997 and 2005 and has continued to assist the development of women's cricket as a coach and commentator and through her work with Cricket Victoria.

Alex Kountouris has been the Australian cricket team physiotherapist since 2006. From 1995 to 2003 he was the head physiotherapist of the Sri Lankan national team during which time the team participated in three World Cups and won the championship in 1996. Between 2003 and 2006 he was the coordinator of the Latrobe University master's degree course in Sports Physiotherapy and is still a sessional lecturer in that program.

Justin Langer AM, scored 23 centuries as a higher-order batsman for Australia in 105 Test matches during an international career from 1993 to 2007. His opening partnership with Matthew Hayden was the most successful in Australian Test cricket history and included six double century stands. He has also played for Middlesex and captained Somerset in the English County League. He was named a Wisden Cricketer of the Year in 2001.

Ashley Mallett played in 38 Test matches and nine One-Day Internationals for Australia between 1968 and 1980. As an off spin bowler, he took 132 Test wickets, including the figures of 8/59 against Pakistan at the Adelaide Oval in 1972. He has coached many of the best and emerging spin bowlers in world cricket and is presently a consultant coach for Sri Lanka.

Rod Marsh MBE, was Australia's wicketkeeper in 96 Test matches and 92 One-Day Internationals between 1970 and 1984. He was involved in 355 Test dismissals, many as part of the famous 'caught Marsh, bowled Lillee' combination and was named a Wisden Cricketer of the Year in 1982. He was head coach at both the Australian and English Cricket Academies between1990 and 2005 and is now director of coaching at the ICC Global Cricket Academy in Dubai.

Christina Matthews represented Victoria, New South Wales and the Australian Capital Territory as a wicketkeeper in an interstate career that spanned 12 seasons. She made her Test debut against India in Delhi in 1984 and played in 20 Test matches and 47 One-Day Internationals. She took 81 catches and made 26 stumpings in her 67 appearances for Australia. Following her retirement as a player, she has worked as an operations manager with Cricket New South Wales and been an assistant coach and selector of the national team.

Brian McFadyen was a first-grade cricketer in Victoria and South Australia between 1985 and 1996, where he excelled as a fast bowler and late-order batsman. He commenced a career in coaching as an assistant coach of the Victorian team before moving to Tasmania in 2002, where he led that state to a Sheffield Shield victory in 2004/05. In 2005 he was appointed to the Cricket Australia Centre of Excellence in Brisbane, where he has specialised in the coaching of safe pace bowling techniques.

Tom Moody played eight Test Matches and 76 One-Day Internationals for Australia. As a higher-order batsman, he scored two Test centuries and was a key player in winning two World Cup finals in 1987 and 1999. He was named a Wisden Cricketer of the Year in 2000. He also played for Warwickshire and was captain of Worcestershire in the English County competition. He coached Sri Lanka in 2005/06 before becoming manager/head coach of the Western Warriors in his home state of Western Australia.

Tim Nielsen was appointed Australia's national coach in 2007. After playing 101 first-class matches for South Australia as a wicketkeeper batsman, he retired in 1999 to be an assistant to coach Greg Chappell with the South Australian Redbacks. Between 2002 and 2005 he was assistant to national coach John Buchanan before becoming head coach at the Cricket Australia Centre of Excellence.

John Orchard is a sports physician who provides injury surveillance consulting services to Cricket Australia and is the senior doctor for New South Wales cricket. He is an adjunct associate professor at the University of Sydney with research interests that include sports injury epidemiology, muscle strains, tendinopathy and ground and surface conditions underlying injury. He has also been the team doctor for professional Australian football and Rugby League teams.

Trevor Penney represented Zimbabwe as an 18-year-old before playing 18 seasons of English County cricket with Warwickshire. He was a middle-order batsman, averaging nearly 40 runs per innings in first-class cricket, as well as an excellent cover fieldsman. Following his retirement as a player in 2005, he became an assistant coach of the Sri Lankan national team before holding a similar position with the Western Warriors in Western Australia.

James Pyke was an all-rounder who played first-grade cricket in Adelaide from 1985 to 2002 and represented South Australia. He was captain/coach of the West Torrens and Sturt clubs for a total of 10 years and then spent a further two years as non-playing coach at Sturt. He is a practicing physiotherapist and presently coaches school and district cricketers in Adelaide.

Carl Rackemann was a tall fast bowler whose career with Queensland spanned 15 years. Between 1982 and 1991 he played in 12 Test matches and 52 One-Day Internationals where he took 39 and 82 wickets, respectively. After his international career was shortened as a result of injury, he retired to coach in Zimbabwe and then became a board member of Queensland Cricket.

Ian Redpath MBE, was a talented and determined opening batsman who played in 66 Test matches for Australia, averaging 43 with eight centuries. He scored three of these centuries in his final Test series against the much-vaunted West Indies pace attack in 1975/76. He was also an outstanding fielder who became vice captain of the team and later coached Victoria to a Sheffield Shield victory.

Greg Shipperd was a top-order batsman with great patience and concentration who played Sheffield Shield cricket for both Western Australia and Tasmania, averaging 42 runs per innings in a career spanning 14 seasons from 1977 to 1991. He then coached Tasmania for 11 seasons, guiding them to their maiden Shield final in 1993/94, and to two subsequent finals, before moving to Victoria and leading that state to two Shield wins in five seasons.

Bob Simpson AO, MBE, was an outstanding all-round cricketer who played in 62 Test matches for Australia between 1957 and 1978 and was named a Wisden Cricketer of the Year in 1965. He averaged 47 runs per innings as an opening batsman, with a highest score of 311, took 71 Test wickets and was one of the best slip fielders in the history of the game. He also captained the team and in 1996 was appointed coach and assisted Australia's revival as a world cricketing power.

Mark Taylor AO, opened the batting for Australia in 104 Test matches during an international career that commenced in 1989 and was highlighted by a mammoth 334 not out against Pakistan. He was also an excellent slip fielder and, after being appointed captain in 1994, was regarded as an adventurous and positive leader. He was named a Wisden Cricketer of the Year in 1990. Since his retirement as a player in 1999, he has become a television cricket commentator and a board member of Cricket Australia.

Martin Tobin has completed a master's degree in education, specialising in sport psychology, at the University of Western Australia. After playing first-grade cricket for the Gosnells and Bayswater-Morley clubs, he has been director of coaching at the University club since 2005. He is involved in the mental skills development of players in Western Australian youth squads and at the Indian Academy of Cricket in Bangalore.

Mike Young is a former professional baseball player who has coached and managed teams affiliated with the Cleveland Indians, Baltimore Orioles and Toronto Blue Jays in North America, as well as being the manager of the Australian baseball team at the 1988 Olympic Games in Seoul. Since 2000 he has been the fielding coach for the Australian cricket team and a coaching consultant to the Cricket Australia Centre of Excellence. He was involved in Australia's 2003 and 2007 World Cup victories.